A collection of
Poems, Songs and Stories
for young children

Wynstones Press

Published by
Wynstones Press
Stourbridge
England.
Email: info@wynstonespress.com
Website: www.wynstonespress.com

First Published 1978 by Wynstones Press
Second edition with music 1983
Fully revised third edition 1999. Reprinted 2005, 2010, 2017

Editors: Jennifer Aulie and Margret Meyerkort

Cover illustration of 'The Tailor' by David Newbatt

© Copyright: Individual contributors and Wynstones Press.
All rights reserved. No part of this publication may be reproduced, stored or transmitted by any means whatsoever without the prior written consent of the publishers.

Typeset by Wynstones Press.
Printed in EU.

British Library CIP data available.

ISBN 9780 946206 476

Summer

This is one in a series of 6 books:
Spring, Summer, Autumn, Winter, Spindrift and Gateways.

The four seasonal books comprise a wide selection of poems, songs and stories appropriate to the time of year, including much material for the celebration of festivals.

Spindrift contains verses and songs describing the world of daily work and practical life, together with a selection of stories from around the world.

Gateways comprises verses and songs for the Morning time, the Evening time and to accompany a variety of traditional Fairytales, together with poems, songs and stories for the celebration of Birthdays.

Warmest thanks to all who have contributed to and supported this work: parents, teachers and friends from Steiner Waldorf Schools in Australia, Britain, Canada, Eire, Estonia, New Zealand, Norway, South Africa and the United States. Grateful thanks also to publishers who have permitted the use of copyright material, acknowledgements for which are at the end of the volume.

INDEX

The Value of Music in the Life of the Young Child . . . 9
Recommended Reading 110

Indexes of first lines
POEMS

A little green frog once lived in a pool	45
A little raindrop here	55
Boom, bang, boom, bang! (the thunderstorm)	59
Clouds are gath'ring once again	56
Dear little violet, open your eye	24
Down in the garden, we'll hoe and rake and sow	41
Ferryman, ferryman row me over	32
Flaming light, shine so bright	21
Grey clouds, grey clouds go away	60
Heaven wears a wondrous crown	30
He creeps and sleeps	46
Hello! Hear the call!	40
Here is the little beehive	53
Here we come a-haying	41
High, high in the bright blue sky	27
I am the cow	45
I am the Sun	32
I'm busy, busy, busy, said the bee	53
In the green meadow some daisies grew	28
I saw a little birdie coming hop, hop, hop	45
It's raining, it's raining	57
Jack and Jill went up the hill	58
Larky, larky, larky lee	27
Little bees work very hard	53
Little brown brother, are you awake in the dark?	28
Little flowers, little flowers, with your colours bright	25
Little Jackie climbs a tree	25
Merrily forth at break of day	39

Mrs. Goose and Mr. Gander	47
Ocean breeze blowing	64
Once I saw a little shell	47
Once I saw an ant hill	54
Once there lived a little girl	34
On the grassy banks	47
Pitter, patter falls the rain	56
Pitter, patter, patter, little drops of rain	54
Poo-poo-pigeons	22
Pretty flower elves are we	58
Put up your umbrella	56
Raindrops, raindrops! Falling all around	54
Sharpen, sharpen well the blade	38
Slip on your raincoat	56
Spirit in rushing wind and air	21
Swing and swing	63
The cow says: Moo!	46
The farmer is busy, so busy today	37
The fleecy sheep	50
The gnome is sitting in his home	60
The goatherd calls his goats together	48
The great sun is setting behind the green hill	31
The hawk flies by so high, so high	43
The rain is raining all around	57
The thunder and lightning they go and they come	60
This is the way we make our hay	40
This little ant went about with a will	54
Two little clouds one sunny day	57
We sing you a story, a wonderful story	38
When the leaves are green, are green	62
Will you help me make a chain	25

SONGS

At Whitsuntide the flowers unfold	22
Ay-a, little bird, softly so you sing	17
Cling, ding, ding, the summer bells now ring	59
Clippety-clap and nickety-nack	61
Dandelion, yellow as gold	29
In and out the bonny bluebells	23
In May I go a-walking	24
In the Summer Garden	26
In the Whitsun Garden	17
King Sun he climbs the Summer sky	30
Little doves so white and free	19
Little Mary Winecups in the hedges grow	51
My pigeon house I open wide	20
Over in the meadow, in the sand, in the sun	42
Run, little goblin	62
Saint John, oh happy festival	33
See a shepherd maiden	48
Sing a song of sunny hours	44
Summer goodbye	64
Summer showers, Summer rain	26
The lark at dawn doth rise from her nest	27
There was a little rose in a garden bed	52
Tomorrow is Midsummer Day	37
We are a big grey cloud just floating in the sky	55
White bird is flying in the sky	18
White sheep, covered with wool	50
Zoom-a-zoom-a-zee, busy, busy bee	53

Index of titles

STORIES

A Bubble Story	88
A Whitsun Daisy Story	65
Elsie and the Seven Sheep	81

In Preparation of Whitsun	67
Midsummer's Eve	75
St. John's Gift	90
The Boy with the Shining Garment	72
The Fairy Weaver	76
The Five Goats	86
The Golden Bucks	94
The Green Button	79
The Sun Castle	102
Whitsun Story	68

The Value of Music in the Life of the Young Child

Free Play in a Waldorf Kindergarten. It is a winter morning: the twenty children are busy with their work. The youngest, three- and four-year-olds, are helping the teacher chop apples for snack; some five-year-old girls are taking care of their "children" in the doll corner; next to them are a group of five-year-old boys and girls who are sitting at a round table polishing stones, grating chestnuts and chatting together. In the centre of the room an observant and energetic four-year-old boy is directing the six-year-olds in the construction of a snowplough: tables are stacked on each other, chairs turned upside down and leaned against the tables for the front part of the plough. A large basket of chestnuts is balanced on top of the plough. The chestnuts are grit and salt, to be scattered later on the ploughed streets. The room is small and the noise level is moderately high.

Underneath the windows, on the carpet where the children have a free space to build up scenes and play with standing puppets and animals, a six-year-old girl sits, absorbed in her work. She has laid out a forest of pine cones, which stands on the banks of a river of blue cloth. Stepping stones allow the poor shepherd boy, who lives at the edge of the forest, to cross the river and wind his way to the castle gates nearby . . . The princess, leaning out of her tower, sees him coming and calls down to him . . .

As she lays out the scene, the girl accompanies her actions with narrative, speaking in a soft tone, sometimes almost whispering to herself. When the puppets begin to live in the scene her voice changes, becoming more sung than spoken, the pitch of her spoken voice being taken over by her singing voice. Her recitative is not sing-song rhythmic, but the rhythm freely moves with the intention of the shepherd boy as he jumps from stone to stone. The pitch of the girl's voice is a colourful monotone: the pitch remains much the same, but the tone colour is enlivened through the intensity and quality of the words as the shepherd crosses the stream. There are moments when a word is spoken, then the narrative is sung again.

When the shepherd arrives at the castle gates, the princess calls down to him from her high tower. She is far away, and the girl reaches up with her voice to the distant place where the princess lives, and sings her greetings down to the shepherd. The girl's voice is high now, but the intervals she sings are not large, they are between a third and a fifth. The high pitch of her voice, although it is not loud, has attracted some of the five-year-olds: several come over to the rug and lie on their stomachs, watching the play unfold. The shepherd now tells the princess of his wish that she come down and go with him. The simple recitative changes to a declamatory aria: a melody of several different tones arises, moving stepwise, the girl's voice becomes more intense as the shepherd pleads his cause. There is little repetition in the melody, but the movement contained in it provides a musical mood which waits expectantly for the princess's reply . . .

In the meantime, the snowplough has already cleared quite a few streets. It has come back to make a second round to scatter the grit and salt . . . The four-year-olds slicing apples jump up from the table. The noise of all those chestnuts hitting a wooden floor is so wonderful, they want to join the fun! The "mothers" putting their children to bed are angry that the snowplough has woken up their little ones, now the babies are crying . . . Some of the children polishing stones and grating chestnuts try throwing their stones and chestnuts on the floor – what a good idea, it makes a lovely *cracking* sound . . .

. . . the five-year-olds listening to the play hold their breaths as the princess agrees to go with the shepherd but he must first ask permission from her father, the king . . . The princess's instructions are sung to him in a melody of seconds with a strong, definite rhythm . . .

An observer can hardly believe that the chestnut-strewn chaos in the other half of the room (which the teacher is quickly helping to put right again) does not seem to penetrate the sheath of peacefulness which surrounds the puppet play. The children gathered around it show no sign that anything else in the room has taken place . . .

At the successful conclusion of the play, the children watching it lie still. The girl covers the scene with a cloth and sings in a half-whispering tone a farewell to the story of the shepherd and the princess. As her voice fades, there is a moment of absolute silence. Then the five-year-olds run back to the polishing table and the girl goes to the teacher to ask how long it will be until snack.

This description of a six-year-old girl's singing contains many elements of what has come to be called "Mood of the Fifth" music: the singing follows the rhythm of speech; melodies are simple, moving within intervals of seconds and thirds – sometimes as large as a fifth, rarely larger; melodies are often sung on one tone, the pitch taken from the speaking voice; the melodies are not written in major or in minor keys and have an open-ended feel to them. Above all is the mood of the music: when sung properly it seems to reach out and enfold the children in a protective sheath which has a quality of stillness and peace, although the children themselves may be active within it.

This music is a musical expression of an experience which is striven for in all aspects of Waldorf Education. It is difficult to describe in words, perhaps: "I am centred in my activity," "My thinking, feeling and willing are in balance." One feels deeply united with a task, at peace and yet still active. The young child finds this mood in play. S/he is deeply engaged in an activity which is then no longer interesting when the activity is over. The moment of silence at the end of the play was not a moment of reflection, but a moment which allowed the activity of watching the play to come to a complete end before the next task could engage the children's attention.

The broader context of this musical experience should be noted: the kindergarten just described is one where mood-of-the-fifth music was not cultivated by the teacher. The children learned only traditional children's songs and games which were sung in strict rhythm, and with major or minor key melodies. The six-year-old girl experienced similar music at home.

Yet the girl's singing is not an isolated or unusual musical event. Such singing can often be heard when a child's attention is fully engaged in his/her play. We grown-ups tend to dismiss such fragments of melody as noise, or incomplete attempts by the child to sing our music, not listening closely enough to discover the innate coherence of the child's activity. Too often well-meaning adults try to "correct" the pitch which is too high, or the rhythm which is irregular, and slowly wall in a living musicality with "proper" songs . . . Sooner or later, often at puberty, an attempt is made at breaking through these walls, as the pounding beat of popular music has long suggested.

The use of "Mood of the Fifth" music in the kindergarten encompasses two considerations. It is first of all a path of musical development for the adult, which schools his/her musical perception and ability so that s/he is able to participate in a musicality which the children *already possess*. This musicality may, for many reasons, lie dormant or misshapen within an individual child or group of children. Through the adult's use of Mood of the Fifth s/he can reawaken and bring back into movement the musicality which is so essential for the full development of the child's soul life. (To be labelled "unmusical" or "tone deaf" causes deep, lingering wounds to the child's self esteem. There are unfortunately many adults who can attest to the truth of this statement out of their own experience.)

Mood of the Fifth music can also help the adult to establish an additional point of contact with the child which shows him/her that the adult *understands*. One of the rewards of working with young children is surely the open look of delight on a child's face when s/he hears a story, plays a game, experiences something which pleases him/her. The look of delight means more, however, than just "I like that." On a deeper level it expresses the child's trust in the adult: "You know who I am, and what you offer me is that which I am searching for with my deepest intentions. I can follow you."

The present day task of the Waldorf Kindergarten is primarily a therapeutic one. It provides children with basic experiences which they need for healthy development, overcoming deficiencies which often occur today in the first years of life. A very large part of these experiences are sensory, as the development of the physical senses (touch, balance, etc.) lays the foundation for the later unfolding of the spiritual capacities (thinking, speech, etc.). The kindergarten is not a mirror of our daily lives, but an extract of the many activities, distilled to their essence. This provides a simplicity and basic necessity for the content of kindergarten life which the child can understand and imitate wholeheartedly. The meaningful activity around the child awakens his/her interest in the world, and this interest becomes the mainspring of later learning.

In the arts the materials presented to the child are restricted to essentials, and with these the child's imagination has free rein. This can be clearly seen, for example, in painting: the three primary colours are used – red, yellow and blue. The children are given watercolours, a large wet sheet of paper and a broad brush to paint with. The materials themselves preclude any precise drawing, colours flow into one another, sometimes mixing, sometimes remaining pure side by side. There is no right or wrong way of using the colours, the expansive, fiery or cool moods of the colours themselves guide the child's brush. The medium of water enables the child's soul to breathe freely in the movement of colour with the brush. If only the paper were bigger s/he could paint on and on . . .

Music can be approached in a similar way. Here as well the materials can be restricted so that the *activity* becomes of foremost importance. Only five different tones of our twelve tone system are used:

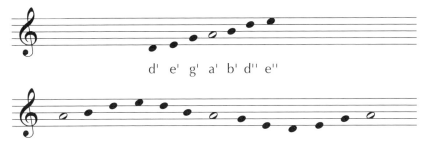

d' e' g' a' b' d'' e''

When a children's harp or lyre is used, the strings are tuned to pure fifths (like a violin's open strings) rather than the tempered intervals of the piano. The songs are not written in major or minor keys, but tend to circle around the middle tone, a'. The rhythm is free, either gently swinging (3 or 6 beats) or walking (2 or 4 beats), but the movement of the music takes its impulse from the words and seeks to accompany its inner content.

This style of music making lends itself wonderfully to the activities of circle time where movement, the spoken word and song freely flow from one to the other, just as the three basic colours do in painting. Teachers who have worked with Mood of the Fifth music in the classroom also know of its effectiveness in creating moments where the attention of all of the children is engaged, enabling a special mood to arise, whether in a puppet play, grace before meal, etc.

Newcomers to this music may at first experience difficulty in hearing the melodies or finding an inner connection to them. Others may have trouble finding the beginning pitch or singing the songs as high as they are written. None of these difficulties should be considered unsolvable problems.

Over time, the practice of Music of the Fifth songs often leads to a good sense of pitch. The voice gradually learns the placement of the tones, and the reduced number of tones make sight-singing possible even for the "unmusical" person.

Difficulty in reaching the higher notes (d", e"), which lie within traditional singing range of soprano and altos, can be due to breathing which is too shallow, as well as to the false idea that high notes are more difficult to sing and require greater effort. In the long run, the question of extending the vocal range is best addressed by an experienced teacher. But those without a teacher can still consider the following: the vocal range can be affected by physical movement. Often much can be accomplished by accompanying a song with large, simple, physical gestures. This helps free the breathing, allowing greater ease in reaching notes which are "too high." The songs can be practised with movement until the feeling of vocal mobility is secure. Then the outward movement can gradually become smaller and disappear altogether, all the while maintaining the inner freedom of movement in the voice.

An essential guide for adults who wish to find a path into the experience of Mood of the Fifth music can be found in Julius Knierim's *Songs in the Mood of the Fifth (Quintenlieder)*. This succinct and clearly written booklet describes, with simple exercises and musical examples, a path which really can be taken by all who have a sincere interest in further development of their musical abilities. By working with the suggestions contained in Julius Knierim's essay, the serious student can develop capacities which not only lead him/her into the musical world of the young child, but can help build a new relationship to traditional classical music, and to all further musical development.

Rudolf Steiner, in discussing music for the young child, spoke of the great importance of the Quintenstimmung = *Mood* of the Fifth. The suggestions mentioned in this article, and most especially in Dr. Knierim's book, are guideposts by which adults may find the way into this mood. They are not the mood itself. Individual observation, experimentation, and practice are the means by which the letter of the law may be enlivened by its spirit.

The goal of these booklets is to offer immediate practical help in working with young children. It is for this reason that a variety of musical styles is included. All songs (as well as stories and verses) have proved their worth in Waldorf kindergartens or other settings with young children. Some traditional tunes with new words have been included, and many traditional rhymes have been set to new melodies (either pentatonic or Mood of the Fifth). Familiar children's songs have been excluded for the most part because these are readily available in other collections. Most songs are set in D-pentatonic. This is done for pedagogical as well as practical reasons (see references). Experience has shown that many teachers and parents who wish to consciously address music-making with the young child are often just those who are themselves struggling with their own musical education. With most songs written in D-pentatonic mode (which are tones of a Choroi flute or children's harp, and are easy to play on a traditional recorder), it is hoped that the initial difficulties with note reading and transposition will be eased. The use of bar lines and time signatures varies, showing new possibilities of notation. Some songs have traditional time signatures, others have only a 3 or 4 at the beginning to indicate a more swinging or walking rhythm. The absence of bar lines leaves the singer free to determine the musical phrasing according to the rhythm of the words and their sense. Commas indicate a slight pause, or point of rest.

Jennifer Aulie

References:

Knierim, Julius. *Songs in the Mood of the Fifth 'Quintenlieder'*.
ISBN 0 945803 14 1 (Rudolf Steiner College Press, California)

Steiner, Rudolf. *The Study of Man*.
ISBN 9781855841871 (Rudolf Steiner Press, England)

Steiner, Rudolf. *The Inner Nature of Music and the Experience of Tone*.
ISBN 9780880100748 (Steiner Books, USA)

M. Bucknall   *M. Bucknall*

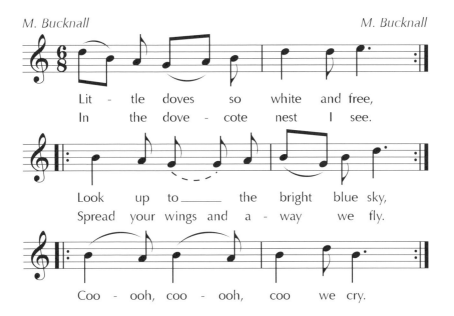

Little doves so white and free,
In the dovecote nest I see.
Look up to the bright blue sky,
Spread your wings and away we fly.
Coo-ooh, coo-ooh, coo we cry.

2. Flutter silently around,
   Lighting gently on the ground,
   Back into the dovecot fly,
   Fold your wings and gladly sigh:
   Coo ooh, coo ooh, here am I,
   Coo ooh, coo ooh, here am I.

Suggested directions:
For the very young: *Adult sits on a low stool with a light blue sheet around her/him, under which the children are sitting. Adult opens her/his arms and the children freely fly around the room. When the 'pigeons' have returned the adult brings her/his arms together.*

Second way: *About half the number of children walk around in a circle and sing the last 4 bars of the song, while the other children crouch in the centre. The circle children stand still, raise arms so that the 'pigeons' can freely fly around the room. When the pigeons have returned to the centre, the circle children lower their arms and walk and sing as at the beginning.*

WHITSUN
Spirit in rushing wind and air,
In sunlight, cloud and rainbow fair,
Spirit in flame and snow white flower,
Oh come to us with mighty power.

W. Doncaster

Flaming light,
Shine so bright,
Flaming light,
Give your might,
Make us strong and make us bold
Turn our word to living gold.

M. Meyerkort

1. Poo-poo-pigeons
   Would you like some peas?
   Here you are and there you are
   As many as you please.

2. Poo-poo-pigeons
   Was your dinner good?
   Here you go and there you go
   And off into the wood.

From Japan

From Scotland   *Traditional Scottish*

In and out the bonny bluebells, in and out the bonny bluebells, in and out the bonny bluebells you shall be my partner. Pitta patta, pitta patta on your shoulder, pitta patta, pitta patta on your shoulder, pitta patta, pitta patta on your shoulder, you shall be my partner.

Suggested directions:

Children stand in a ring with arms raised to form arches. Two children, or an adult, go in and out of the arches and at each 'Pitta-patta-pitta-patta' touch a child's shoulder who will then follow the leader.

Dear little violet, open your eye,
Bright is the sun, and blue the sky.

N. B. Hartford

Little Jackie climbs a tree,
So high you can no longer see.
From bough to bough goes on his quest
And now he's at the pigeon's nest.
Ah-ha! laughs Jack – – –
The bough goes crack –
And down! He falls onto the grass.

From Germany

1. Little flowers, little flowers,
    With your colours bright,
    Look above now to the sky,
    Full of warmth and light.

2. Praise the lovely golden sun,
    He who gave you birth,
    Little flowers, fallen stars,
    Shining on the earth.

Will you help me make a chain,
Of yellow, green and white?
Then follow me down twisty lanes,
Through a field of daisies bright.
One by one we gather them,
Then in the oak tree's shade
We gently thread them stem to stem
And see a daisy chain we've made.

H. Henley

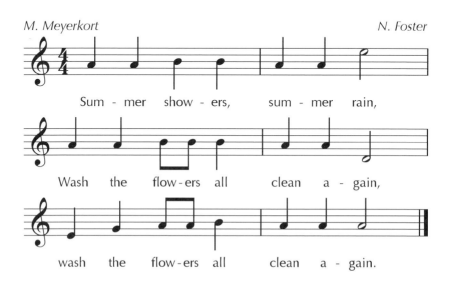

Larky, larky, larky, lee,
Who'll go up to heaven with thee?
Never a lad who lies in bed,
Nor a sulky girl who hangs her head.
Up into the air we go,
Tee-hee, tee-hee, tee-hee.

High, high in the bright blue sky,
Floating and trilling the lark doth fly.
Higher and higher the blue he wings,
Louder and sweeter he trills and sings.
Low, low, deep down below,
Where cool green grasses and winged flowers blow,
On Mother Earth's breast the baby larks rest.
Down flies the lark to his babes in the nest.
Where have you been to, lark so high?
What did you see in the bright blue sky?
I heard an angel sweetly sing.
I heard the morning bells all ring.

Traditional M. Winship

The lark at dawn doth rise from her nest, And mounts in the air with dew-ey breast.

2. And like the ploughboy she whistles and sings
At night in her nest she sleeps again.

Little brown brother, oh, little brown brother
Are you awake in the dark?
Here we lie cosily, close to each other,
Hark, to the song of the lark.
Waken, the lark says, and dress you,
Put on your green coat and gay
Blue sky will shine on you, sunshine caress you,
Waken, 'tis morning, 'tis May!
Little brown brother, oh, little brown brother,
What kind of flower will you be?
I'll be a poppy, all red like my mother,
Do be a poppy like me.
What? You're a sunflower? How I shall miss you,
When you are golden and high,
But I shall send all the bees up to kiss you,
Little brown brother, goodbye!

In the green meadow some daisies grew,
Hiding their faces away from the dew.
When all of a sudden the sun came out,
With a big warm heart and a merry shout.
Lift up your heads, he loudly cried.
The daisies opened their petals wide.
Then into the grasses a warm wind blew-
The daisies nodded as the breeze passed through.
Came a little girl to the meadow to play
And said, "I'll make me a garland today."
So she gathered some daisies that grew in the sun
And strung them together one by one.

2. Dandelion, yellow as gold,
   What do you do all night?
   I wait and I wait in the long green grass,
   Till my hair grows long and white.

3. What do you do when your hair grows white
   And the children come to play?
   They take me up in their dimpled hands
   And blow my hair away.

Heaven wears a wondrous crown,
Lit with thousand jewels bright
And in streaming, magic light
Thousand stars are dancing down.
Dark in ground we rest-and grow
Into flowers' wondrous glow.
Lily, rose and bluebell hold
Magic mantle of red and gold.
Little flower, fallen star,
Shining on the earth afar.

M. Meyerkort

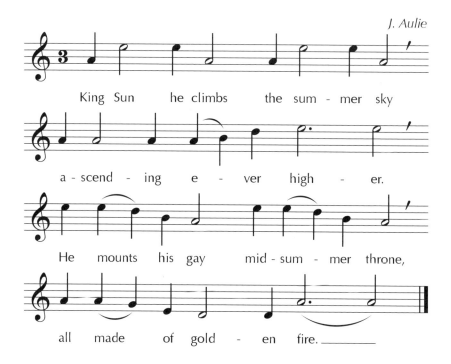

J. Aulie

King Sun he climbs the sum-mer sky
a-scend-ing e-ver high-er.
He mounts his gay mid-sum-mer throne,
all made of gold-en fire.

2. His flowing mantle, flowing free,
His shining gifts he showers
All golden on the earth and sea,
On men and beasts and flowers.

1. The great sun is setting behind the green hill.
   The flowers are sleeping the meadow is still.
   Only the night wind so gentle and light
   Now stirs the tall grasses and whispers goodnight.

2. The great sun is rising above the green hill.
   His golden light gleaming on meadow and rill.
   He shines on the flowers, they wake one by one
   And spread out their petals to greet the great sun.

3. They dance in the sunshine to greet the bright day.
   They dance in the sunshine so blithe and so gay.
   The violets all curtsey, the bluebells ring sweet.
   The daisies all twirl round in skirts white and neat.

4. The great moon is rising above the green hill.
   Her silver beams shining on meadow and rill.
   She shines on the fairies, they wake here and there
   And spread out their wings to dance in the air.

5. The great moon is setting behind the green hill.
   The fairies are sleeping, the meadow is still.
   Only the morning wind gentle and gay
   Doth stir the tall grasses and whisper good-day.

I am the Sun –
And I bear with my might
The earth by day, the earth by night.
I hold her fast, and my gifts I bestow
To everything on her, so that it may grow:
Man and stone, flower and bee
All receive their light from me.
Open thy heart, dear child, to me,
That we together one light may be.

                Ch. Morgenstern

Ferryman, ferryman row me over,
Row me over,
Row me over,
Out of the earth to the land of the sun.
Elves and dwarfs and gnomes and pixies,
Gnomes and pixies,
Gnomes and pixies,
Follow their path to the land of the sun.
Water sprites, sylphs and fire fairies gleaming,
Fire fairies gleaming,
Fire fairies gleaming,
Follow their path to the land of the sun.
See the sun is shining, turning,
Golden burning,
Shining, turning.
Over the earth on Midsummer's Day.

                M. Bucknall

M. Geuter J. Aulie

St. John, oh happy festival,
Thou festival of light,
With songs and happy melodies
Our souls may grow so wide.

2. For all the beauty of the world
   Which loving spirits have unfurled,
   Oh come! Oh come ye spirits gay
   And dance with us on Saint John's Day.

THE FAIRY WEAVER

Once there lived a little girl
And Eileen was her name,
Her mother wove the finest cloth
And father kept the farm.

In the morning Eileen woke
Skipped barefoot on the floor,
And ran to feed the little mice
Who lived beneath the door.

Out she went into the yard
To find a hazel twig,
To scratch and scratch the muddy backs
Of every little pig.

Then it was time to sweep and clean
While mother wove and spun,
Then in the meadow out to play
When all the work was done.

One day the sun was shining down
As brightly as he could,
And Eileen trailed the butterflies
That fluttered in the wood.

On and on she followed 'till
A babbling brook she found,
And as she listened to its song
She heard a little sound.

A tiny man stood there, "Oh dear
Whatever shall I do?
My shuttle's fallen in the brook
And I'm too small to go."

Continued...

"I'll fetch it for you," Eileen said,
 And quickly waded in.
"Thank you kindly, Eileen dear,
Now I can weave again."

"If you need help then call," he said,
And sat down to his loom.
Weaving the silken spider threads
That like the rainbow shone.

The next day father drove the cart
To market in the town,
To fetch the man to buy the cloth
That mother wove and spun.

Eileen waved him on his way
But mother was feeling ill,
"Lie down to rest and sleep awhile
And soon you will be well."

An angel watched by mother's bed
As fast asleep she lay,
And Eileen crept out of the house
Along the forest way.

And little man was weaving still
All on his tiny loom,
"Mother is ill, and who will weave
Her cloth until it's done?"

"Do not fear," the weaver said
"Go home and sleep today,
Tomorrow morning when you wake
You'll see what you will see."

Continued...

In the morning when the sun
Was shining through the door,
Mother was well and all the cloth
Lay finished on the floor.

"Whose work is this, my daughter dear?
Oh, who can weave so fine?"
"It was the little weaver man
Who sits beside the stream."

"One of the fairy folk it was
Who helped us all today,
Go thank him kindly, Eileen dear,
Run quickly, do not stay."

J. Mehta

THE FAIRY WEAVER

J. Mehta

J. Aulie

To - mor - row is Mid - sum - mer Day.
The spir - its of light all dance and play.
So join your hands and let us sing:
The sun, he is our shin - ing king!

The farmer is busy, so busy today,
Trying to gather in all his hay.
So off to the hayfield hurry away
And see what we can do.

We rake and toss and turn the hay,
We pile up the rick as high as we may,
We ride in the cart which takes it away,
There is so much to do.

E. Adams

We sing you a story, a wonderful story,
We sing you a story of Midsummer Night.
For all who would know of the dance of the fairies,
For all who would seek for the rose of light.
We gather the blossom, to twine in our hair.
We sip of the honey, the golden honey,
We sip of the honey, so sweet and rare.
We go to the fountain, the sparkling fountain.
We go to the fountain for water fair.
The wind in the fountain, the sparkling fountain,
Has stirred the water that floweth fair.
We taste of the water, the sparkling water,
The living water, that floweth fair.
And there in the twilight the fairies are dancing,
The fairies are dancing as light as air.
They lead to the garden, the Midsummer Garden,
They lead to the garden, where roses bloom.
The flowers are singing, are swaying and singing,
The flowers are singing with stars and with moon.
And there is the Mother, the white robed Mother,
The Mother of all who shines in light.
She gives us a rose from her garland of roses,
She gives us a rosebud so pure and white.
Oh, guard it forever the beautiful blossom,
Oh, guard it forever the rose of light.

E. Hutchins

Sharpen, sharpen well the blade,
Up and down the whetstone pass.
Sharpen, sharpen, up and down.
Sharpen it to cut the grass.

M. Meyerkort

1. Merrily forth at break of day,
   All in the Midsummer sun,
   Into the meadow to mow the hay,
   There we will have some fun.

2. We swing our scythes so blithe and gay,
   All in the Midsummer sun,
   We'll cut and hew, we'll swish and sway,
   Till our work is done.

3. We toss the grass so long and fair,
   All in the Midsummer sun,
   Its fragrance fills the sunlit air,
   Till the day is done.

4. Briskly into haycocks steep,
   All in the Midsummer sun,
   The dry and fragrant hay we'll keep
   Till our work is done.

5. Slowly home we wind our way,
   All in the Midsummer sun,
   Glad are we at the end of day,
   That our work is done.

6. Then let us all my merry men
   Thank the sun on high,
   For all the gifts he showers on us
   As he circles through the sky.

1. Hello! Hear the call!
   It's haying time for all!
   Come lads, and come lasses,
   And rake up the grasses!
   The scythe clears the way,
   Now haste and make the hay!

2. The sun wears a crown,
   And pours his glory down;
   The dew-drops he's drinking,
   And laughs while he's blinking
   With each burning ray,
   The green is turned to grey.

3. Hello! Hear the call!
   The hayrack waits for all!
   So homeward we're hieing,
   For rain-clouds are flying.
   Hurrah for the day
   We've made the fragrant hay!

                      K. Forman

This is the way we make our hay;
Men cut the grass, then lad and lass,
We take it and shake it, and shake it,
Then into heaps we rake it,
And leave it to the sun to bake it;
And when it is brown we pull it down,
And again we take it and shake it,
And again with our rakes we rake it;
And when we have done with dance and fun,
Home in our carts we take it.

                    A. Craves

Here we come a-haying
A-haying, a-haying,
Here we come a-haying
Among the leaves so green.

Up and down the mower goes
All the long field over
Cutting down the long green grass
And the purple clover.

Toss the hay and turn it
Laid in rows so neatly
Summer sun a-shining down
Makes the grass smell sweetly.

Rake it into tidy piles.
Now the farmer's ready
Load it on his old hay-cart
Pulled by faithful Neddy.

Down the lane the last load goes
Hear the swallow calling
Now at last our work is done
Night-is softly falling.

E. Close

1. Down in the Garden, we'll hoe and rake and sow,
   Down in the garden, we'll hoe and rake and sow,
   Then in the warm sun the seeds will grow,
   Down in the garden, we'll hoe and rake and sow.

2. Down in the garden, we'll pull and pull the weeds,
   Down in the garden, we'll pull and pull the weeds,
   Then in the warm sun the seeds will grow,
   Down in the garden, we'll pull and pull the weeds.

L. M. Fox

2. Over in the meadow where the stream runs so blue,
   Lives a dear mother fish and her little fishes two.
   Swim, says the mother, we swim, say the two,
   So they swim and they swim where the stream runs so blue.

3. Over in the meadow in the big oak tree,
   Lives a dear mother robin and her little robins three.
   Fly, says the mother, we fly, say the three,
   So they fly, and they fly round the big oak tree.

Continued...

4. Over in the meadow in the reeds by the shore,
   Lives a mother water rat and her little ratties four.
   Dive, says the mother, we dive, say the four,
   So they dive and they dive in the reeds by the shore.

5. Over in the meadow in a sunny beehive,
   Lives a mother honey bee and her little bees five.
   Buzz, says the mother, we buzz, say the five,
   So they buzz and they buzz in the sunny beehive.

6. Over in the meadow in a nest built of sticks.
   Lives a dear mother crow and her little crows six.
   Caw, says the mother, we caw, say the six,
   So they caw and they caw in their nest built of sticks.

7. Over in the meadow where the grass is so even,
   Lives a dear mother cricket and her little crickets seven.
   Chirp, says the mother, we chirp, say the seven,
   So they chirp and they chirp where the grass is so even.

The hawk flies by so high, so high,
He's just a speck against the sky.
But when he comes, the Mother Hen
Calls all her chicks to wing again.
She watches with an anxious eye
Until the hawk has circled by,
Nor lets the chicks run out to play
Until the hawk has flown away.

A. Riley

A little green frog once lived in a pool,
The sun was so hot, and the water so cool.
He stayed in the pool the whole day long,
Singing his dear little, queer little song.
Quaggery, quaggery, quaggery dee,
No-one was ever so happy as me.

R. Fyleman

1. I saw a little birdie coming hop, hop, hop,
   And I said, little bird won't you stop, stop, stop?
   Won't you stop a moment and play with me?
   But he wagged his little tail and away flew he.

2. I saw a little fish come swimming past,
   And I said, little fish why do you swim so fast?
   Can't you stop a moment and play with me?
   But he wagged his little tail and swam down to the sea.

3. I saw a big, big cow saying moo, moo, moo,
   And I said, big, big cow what do you do, do, do?
   Can't you come a minute and play with me?
   I am busy eating grass to make milk for your tea.

I am the cow
I say moo-moo
I give you milk
And butter too.

I. Tupaj

1. The cow says: Moo!
   And looks at you.
   The cow says: moo!
   How do you do?

2. The horse says: neigh!
   I will not stay.
   The horse says: neigh: neigh!
   And runs away.

3. The dog says: bow-wow!
   We shall have a row.
   The dog says: bow-wow!
   I want a bone now.

   I. Tupaj

SNAIL POEM

He creeps
And sleeps
Among the heaps
Of fallen leaves.....

The tiny snail
His slimy tail
A shiny trail
Behind him leaves.

E. Simon

Once I saw a little shell
Upon a garden wall.
I tapped upon the little door.
No answer came at all.
But as I turned to go away,
A snail crept out to see
Who tapped upon his little door,
And waved his horns at me.

On the grassy banks
Lambkins at their pranks;
Woolly sisters, woolly brothers
Playing by their woolly mother.
Scamper with their feet
Hear them softly bleat.

C. Rossetti

1. Mrs. Goose and Mr. Gander
   Like to wander and meander,
   Through the fields they like to stray,
   Eating grasses all the day.

2. Now they waddle down the lane,
   Back they wander home again;
   Sunny days or rainy weather,
   They must take their work together.

N. K. Duffy

1. The goatherd calls his goats together
   For a walk in Summer weather.
   Then stepping over stones I go.
   Stepping high and stepping low.

2. I'll take you through the mountain gate:
   The billies hold their heads so straight.
   Then skipping, skipping off they go,
   Skipping high and skipping low.

3. I'll take you to the drinking well:
   The nannies nodding ring their bell.
   Then trotting, trotting off they go,
   Trotting high and trotting low.

4. I'll take you where the grass is sweet:
   The kiddies twirl their tail and bleat.
   Then tip-toe, tip-toe off they go,
   Tip-toe high and tip-toe low.

5. I'll take you to the hollow tree
   And now to rest, lie down by me.

                              M. Meyerkort

Continued...

Suggested directions:

Half the participants form a circle and walk around, while the other half walk around outside the circle.

At 'gate': circle children raise arms and 'sheep' walk in and out under the arches.

For the last line 'sheep' crouch down in centre. They then get up to become the new 'gate'.

1. The fleecy sheep,
   They run and leap,
   Among the ferns and grasses deep
   They leap and run,
   And in the sun,
   They're quite contented, ev'ry one.
   Oh Shepherdess fair,
   Oh Shepherdess fair,
   Give your sheep the best of care!

2. I'd like to keep
   A flock of sheep,
   To have as pets, like Miss Bo Peep;
   I'd help them creep
   Where paths were steep,
   But oh, I'd never fall asleep!
   Oh Shepherdess say,
   Oh Shepherdess say,
   Have you counted them today?

Mary Winecups is the colloquial name for the pink-striped convolvulus.

From Germany N. Foster

2. There came a little bee and he said: "Zoom, zoom!'
   Hey – ho! Le the winds blow!
   I'd like a drop of gold, pretty rosy bloom.
   Hey – ho! Let the winds blow!

3. There came a little bird and he said: "Tweet, tweet!'
   Hey – ho! Let the winds blow!
   I sing a merry song for my lady sweet.
   Hey – ho! Let the winds blow!

4. There came a little girl and she danced and said,
   Hey – ho! Let the winds blow!
   I love my little rose with her petals so red.
   Hey – ho! Let the winds blow!

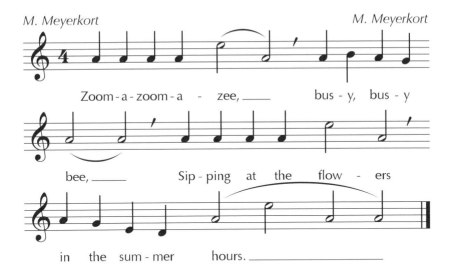

Here is the little beehive.
Where are the bees?
Hidden away where nobody sees.
Soon they come creeping out of the hive.
One, two, three, four, five.

I'm busy, busy, busy, said the bee,
I shan't be home for dinner or tea,
It takes me hours and hours
To visit all the flowers.

Little bees work very hard,
Making golden honey,
Taking nectar from the flowers,
When the days are sunny.

Once I saw an anthill
With no ants about.
So I said, "Dear little ants,
Won't you come out?"
Then, as if the little ants
Had heard my call,
One, two, three, four, five came out!
And that was all.

This little ant went about with a will
Gathering firewood, till, till, till
A shower came and caught it!
To its little house it hurries;
In its little hill it scurries.

From Mexico

Pitter, patter, patter,
Little drops of rain
Tap against my window,
Splash upon the pane.

J. Hoover

Raindrops, raindrops!
Falling all around.
Pitter-patter on the chimney,
Pitter-patter on the ground!
Here is my umbrella.
It will keep me dry.
When I'm walking in the rain
I hold it up so high.

A little raindrop here,
A little raindrop there,
Many raindrops pitter, patter
And the clouds are everywhere.

H. Bedyn

Slip on your raincoat,
Pull on galoshes;
Wading in puddles
Makes splishes and sploshes!

Put up your umbrella,
There's rain in the sky.
Put up your umbrella
To keep yourself dry!
Pitter, patter, pitter, patter,
Softly it falls.
Hurry home quickly
Before Mother calls.

Pitter, patter falls the rain,
On the roof and window pane.
Softly, softly it comes down,
Makes a stream that runs around.
Flowers lift their heads and say:
"A nice cool drink for us today."

Clouds are gath'ring once again,
Bustling in to talk of rain.
Water-drops are falling down
On the fields and on the town.

H. Bedyn

Two little clouds one sunny day,
Went flying through the sky,
They went so fast, they bumped their heads
And both began to cry.
Old Father Sun looked out and said:
"Oh, never mind my dears,
I'll send my little fairy folk
To dry your fallen tears."
One came in pink and one in red,
The next in orange bright.
In yellow, green, blue, violet,
They made a pretty sight.
They changed the rolling, crying tears
To drizzling drops of fun,
And then the fairies laughed and said:
"We thank you, rain and sun."

The rain is raining all around
It falls on field and tree,
It rains on the umbrellas here
And on the ships at sea.

R. L. Stevenson

It's raining, it's raining,
It's raining hard today
And when the earth has had enough
The rain will stop and stay.

M. Meyerkort

1. Pretty flower elves are we
   Dancing to and fro,
   Peeping out from 'neath our buds
   As round and round we go.

2. Sleepy, sleepy snails are we
   Our steps are long and slow.
   We drag our feet along the ground
   As round and round we go.

3. Butterflies from the air are we
   Our wings are fairy light.
   We dance before the king and queen
   Upon the flowers bright.

4. Funny little gnomes are we
   Our beards are long and white
   Towards the rocks our footsteps turn
   To tap from morn 'til night.

5. A long green snake in the grass are we
   Our tail is far away.
   We wriggle and wriggle and twist and turn
   As in and out we sway.

    Jack and Jill went up the hill
    And down in pouring rain-Oh.
        Off they spring and laugh and sing
        And here they come again-Oh.
    Up they run and full of fun
    They meet Sir Tommy Tucker.
        Jack and Jill high up the hill
        Come down and have some supper.

M. Meyerkort.

From Germany   *Traditional German*

Cling, ding, ding, The summer bells now ring: There's laughter on the hills, The daisies show their frills. Cling, ding, ding, Be welcome, Summer King!

2. Cling, ding, ding,
   The summer bells now ring:
   The shepherd pipes all day,
   The lambkins frisk and play.
   Cling, ding, ding,
   Be welcome Summer King.

Boom, bang, boom, bang!
Rumpety, lumpety, bump!
Zoom, zam, zoom, zam!
Clippety, clappety, clump!
Rustles and bustles
And swishes and zings!
What wonderful noises
A thunderstorm brings!

The thunder and lightning they go and they come,
But the stars and the stillness are always at home.

Grey clouds, grey clouds go away
Les us see the sun today.

The gnome
Is sitting in his home:
Methinks I hear
Some raindrops near:
Drop, drop, drop, drop
Drizzle on the treetop.

The gnome
Is sitting in his home:
Methinks I hear
Some raindrops near:
Rain, rain, rain, rain
Back into my house again.

The gnome
Is sitting in his home:
Methinks I hear
Some raindrops near:
Storm, storm, storm, storm
Quickly, quickly back I turn.

M. Meyerkort

Run, lit-tle gob-lin, Run a-long to mar-ket,
Run a-long to mar - ket, Buy me a cow.

2. Gold, little goblin?
   Not a penny have I!
   Make it by your magic,
   Buy me a cow.

3. Buy me a brown cow
   And a stool for milking
   And a little bucket
   Too, for the cream.

4. Run, little goblin,
   Run along to market,
   Run along to market,
   Buy me a cow.

When the leaves are green, are green
The King will want you for his queen.
When the leaves are brown, are brown
The King will give you a golden crown.

From China

Swing and swing,
Sing and sing,
I'm on the wing.
Low and high,
Here I fly,
Into the sky.
Up and down,
Up and down,
To London Town.
Where, oh, where,
In the air;
Now I'm there.
Soon, so soon,
Afternoon,
O'er sun and moon.
Far, so far,
O'er the bar,
From star to star.
To and fro,
Lower, low,
Down I go.
Slow, so slow,
To and fro,
Grass under my toe.

1. Ocean breeze blowing,
   Feet kick and splash,
   Ocean waves breaking
   On rocks with a crash.

2. Boys finding seashells,
   Girls sifting sand,
   Friends building castles
   As high as they can.

3. I stretch my arms out
   Far as they'll reach.
   Oh, my! What fun
   On this day at the beach.

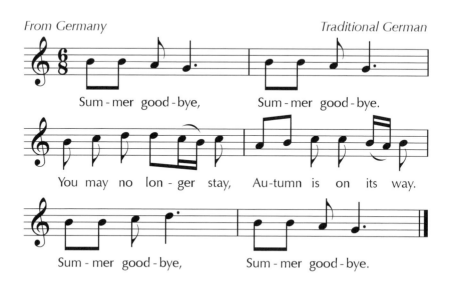

From Germany — Traditional German

Sum-mer good-bye, Sum-mer good-bye.
You may no lon-ger stay, Au-tumn is on its way.
Sum-mer good-bye, Sum-mer good-bye.

A Whitsun Daisy Story

Once there lived a little white flower in the meadow. Her name was 'Daisy'. She longed to fly or run like other creatures but she could not, for her roots grew into the earth and held her there. So she hung her head.

One day she heard singing:

> Rook-a-dee-goo, zeet-zeet-zeee,
> Raise your head and look at me.

The daisy raised her head and saw a white dove sitting on a branch above. His feathers were shining like the sun and his eyes were twinkling like candles.

"Oh, white dove," said the little daisy, "how beautiful you are."

"I am glad that I make you raise your head," said the dove, "but I cannot stay here with you always, for I have to visit many other creatures. Why had you hung your head?"

"Well," said the daisy, "I am trapped here on the earth. I have no wings to fly with and no legs to run with, and so I have no friends and nothing to do in the world."

"You are a flower and a child of Mother Earth," said the dove, "and you have plenty to do in the world for you have to hold a gift from Father Sun, a golden treasure which you can share with the bees and butterflies."

"How can I find the golden treasure? I cannot fly to Father Sun and fetch it?"

Said the dove: "I will fetch it for you. Open your petals as wide as you can, then you will be ready to receive the golden treasure when I bring it to you."

The white dove flew into the sky, up and up he flew. And the daisy stretched her petals wide open and began to sing:

> "Rook-a-dee-goo, zeet-zeet-zeee,
> White little dove fly here to me."

Soon the dove returned. He was carrying in his beak a tiny flame, a golden flame from Father Sun to himself.

The dove hovered above the daisy and gently laid the tiny flame upon her. At once, there appeared a heart of brightest gold among her petals and the daisy knew she would always hold her head up and give of her gold to bees and butterflies.

H. Mitchell

Henrietta Mitchell wrote this story after studying Rudolf Steiner's lectures on the Whitsun festival, the following paragraph being particularly inspiring. Please feel free to use this story as a framework and adapt it to suit your particular children.

"Whitsun is pre-eminently a festival of flowers. If a person has a true feeling for this Festival he will go out among the buds and blossoms opening under the influence of the sun, under the etheric and astral influences, and he will perceive on the flower-decked earth the earthly image of what flows together in the picture of Christ's Ascension, and the descent of the tongues of fire upon the heads of the disciples which followed later. The heart of the human being as it opens may be symbolised by the flower opening itself to the sun; and what pours down from the sun: giving the flower the fertilising power it needs, may be symbolised by the tongues of fire descending upon the heads of the disciples. Anthroposophy can work upon human hearts with the power that streams from an understanding of the festival times and from true contemplation of each festival season; it can help to evoke the mood-of-soul that conforms truly with these days of the Spring festivals."

Rudolf Steiner – 'The Whitsun' Mystery

In Preparation of Whitsun

Next Sunday is Whitsunday, the Whitsuntide Festival. For hundreds of years it has been called White Sunday because it is a very special day: people know that it is a good and holy day – a day so good and so pure that they call it white.

Still today, in some lonely villages, people do what everyone did, when our grandmothers and grandfathers were little girls and boys, and that was that the cottages were newly painted in dazzling white. And the children had new clothes for White Sunday – not only dresses and suits, but vests and pants, shorts and petticoats too, ties and hair ribbons. And in time for White Sunday the children gathered flowers, white and yellow flowers, made daisy and buttercup chains. Then on White Sunday everything in cottages and country was shining and white, and people sat down together and waited for the oldest man in the village to rise and speak . . . . . and now, we shall have to wait until he has risen from his chair, and then we shall know what he spoke on White Sunday.

E. Hutchins

Whitsun Story

Once upon a time there lived a king who had thirteen sons. One day the twelve older ones set off to seek their fortune, but the thirteenth son stayed at home. He was too young to accompany his brothers.

On twelve fine horses the twelve brothers rode out into the wide world. They came into a country which was covered far and wide with rock and stone, with boulder and bone. There they saw an old woman sitting on the ground and stroking her knees. But the twelve princes were so busy guiding their horses round and over the stones that they had no time to speak to the old woman.

They rode on and came into a country which was covered far and wide with pond and pool, with marsh and moor. There they saw an old woman up to her hips in a swamp. But the princes were so busy guiding their horses round and about the waterways that they had no time to speak to the old woman.

Again, they rode on and came into a country where wind and air were roaring and racing so that they had to hold on to their hats and clothes and even had to hold on to their horses or they would have been blown off and away. They saw an old woman who came rushing, almost flying along, her skirts blown over her head and hanging on to an umbrella which had blown inside out. It looked as if at any moment the old woman would be whisked off into the sky. But the twelve princes were so busy guiding their horses through the rushing air and wind that they had no time to speak to the old woman.

Still they rode on and came at last to a castle. The walls were crumbling, stones were missing, the whole building seemed held together by the ivy which covered it all and was even creeping over the windows. The brothers were thirsty after their long journey and went to the well in the courtyard to draw water. But the well was dry, not a drop could they get to quench their thirst. They went inside the castle. It was dark everywhere from the ivy over the windows, and it was stuffy and damp too. They tried to throw open the windows, but they were rusted over and would not budge. The eldest prince broke the glass in one but at once an old wooden shutter clanged to and sealed it up again, making it darker than ever. The princes came to the banqueting hall. There was a long table laid with food and drink, and decorated with white and gold flowers and twelve candles. The plates and goblets were of gold. The king of the castle was sitting on his throne at the head of the table wearing his golden crown but was fast asleep. The princes tried to wake him but could not. It now became so dark that they could hardly see what they were doing. They tried to light the candles on the table but they just spluttered and went out. So they sat down on twelve chairs round the table and prepared to eat in the dark. But before they could have a bite they became drowsy, and grew drowsier and drowsier until they had fallen fast asleep.

Now when the twelve princes failed to return home, their youngest brother went to his father, the king, and begged to be allowed to go and look for his brothers. At first the king was not willing, he did not want to part with his only remaining son – but at last, he gave permission. Then the youngest prince rode out rejoicing.

He came to a country which was covered far and wide with rock and stone, with boulder and bone. There he saw an old woman sitting on the ground and stroking her knees. The youngest prince stopped his horse and said: "Can I help you?"

"Ah," said the old woman, "I have fallen and hurt my knees."

At once the prince dismounted, went to her and bound up her knees. And he lifted her on to his horse and took her to her cottage. Then the old woman thanked him and said: "Take this little lump of clay. With it you will be able to mend any broken stone and bone." The prince tucked the beautiful gift away carefully, said goodbye to the old woman and went on his way.

Next he came into a country which was covered far and wide with pond and pool, with marsh and moor. There he saw an old woman up to her hips in a swamp. The youngest prince stopped his horse and asked: "Can I help you?"

"Ah," said the old woman, "I am stuck in this water and cannot get out."

At once the prince dismounted and went wading and jumping from tussock to tussock until he reached the old woman. He hoisted her to his shoulders and when he had brought her back safely the old woman thanked him and said: "Take this little bottle of water. With it you will be able to quench many a thirst." The prince tucked the beautiful gift away carefully, said goodbye to the woman and went on his way.

After travelling for some time, he came into a country where wind and air were roaring and racing so that he had to hold on to his hat and clothes and even had to hold on to his horse, or he would have been blown off and away. He saw an old woman who came rushing, almost flying along, her skirts blown over her head and hanging on to an umbrella which had blown inside out. It looked as if at any moment the old woman would be whisked off into the sky. The youngest prince stopped his horse and asked: "Can I help you?"

"Ah," said the old woman, "I cannot stop and stay!"

The prince rode after her and, before another gust of wind came, grabbed hold of her and took her to the shelter of a nearby tower. Then the old woman thanked him and said: "Take this little oil lamp. Its light will make you see wherever you may be." The prince tucked the beautiful gift away carefully, said goodbye to the woman and went on his way.

He came at last to a castle. The walls were crumbling, stones were missing, the whole building seemed held together by the ivy which covered it all and was even creeping over the windows. Then he remembered the gift of the old woman and got out the little lump of clay. He smeared it over the first crack in the wall and instantly it was mended. Then the prince went on filling in holes with his little lump of clay, until the whole stonework of the castle was once more strong and beautiful.

Being thirsty the prince went to the well in the courtyard, but it was dry. Then he remembered the gift of the old woman and took out the little bottle of water. He poured the precious content into the well and instantly water sprang up, and more and more, until the well was filled and the waterfall and stream flowed again. The prince bent down, drank of the living water and was refreshed.

Then the prince went inside the castle. It was stuffy and damp, and it was dark too, from the ivy over the windows. He remembered the gift of the old woman and got out the little oil lamp. It shone and lit up the path in front of him until he reached the banqueting hall. There he found his twelve brothers seated around the table, fast asleep and the king of the castle, at one end of the table, fast asleep too. He tried to wake them but could not: no call, no caress made them stir. Then he saw in the midst of the golden plates, the golden goblets, and the white and golden flowers, the twelve white candles. With the help of his little oil lamp, the thirteenth prince lit them one by one. And when he had lit all twelve, the windows opened and through one window a snow white dove flew in, and settled on the young prince's shoulder. Then the twelve brothers and the enchanted king woke up. They rose to welcome the thirteenth prince and thanked him for freeing them from enchantment. Then they ate and drank together and the thirteen princes went home to their father and there was much rejoicing.

W. Doncaster

The Boy with the Shining Garment

There was once a boy who lived in a most beautiful garden. It was surrounded by stately trees and the air was full of the song of birds. Streams, crystal clear, flowed through the grass, and butterflies of many colours hovered over the flowers. He also had companions, who, like himself, wore white shining garments. He was very happy and he lived on the fruit from the garden. Sometimes his shining companions talked to him. One day one of them said: "The time has come for you to leave us. I will take you to the edge of the garden. Do you see the valley below? It is certainly not very distinct, but that is where you have to go, and you will see it all more clearly as you go down. Your garments are white and clean and shining. Remember to keep them so. And remember, too, that wherever you go and whatever you do we shall always watch you, and you must remember us." So the boy said farewell and started off on the journey. It was quite pleasant at first, just like the garden he had left. But when he had been going downhill for a time, he hit his foot against a rock. It was the first time that he had felt anything but the cool green grass. However, he went on, more carefully now because he began to see more and more stones in the ground and indeed he started to come to patches where there was no grass at all, only stones and dust. Every now and then he remembered his bright, shining companions and looked back to them and could see them smiling at him. As he went on he grew weary and dusty and then he came to a spring which gushed forth from the mountainside. He knelt down gratefully, drank and washed his face and hands and felt refreshed.

Then he went on down into the valley. The way grew rougher and stonier and dustier. Once a briar came across his path and his garments got caught in it. As he freed them he noticed that they were dusty at the hem. He went on and before long he reached the floor of the valley. He saw that there were a lot of people all travelling along in the same direction. By now he was beginning to feel footsore, the road was stony and there was no longer any grass. His feet were cut and sometimes he hardly knew how to go on. Occasionally he remembered and looked back and there he could still see, high up and far away in the distance, his beautiful, shining companions. But they were so far away that he could no longer see whether they were smiling.

Then, when he had been walking for a time, helping his fellow travellers as he went, a man started walking by his side, and he said: "You will find this road almost impossible unless you have a stout pair of shoes. Would you like to come home with me and I will make you a pair?" He had such a kind face that the youth agreed to go home with him and to stay with him until the shoes were ready. When he put them on he felt far more confident, so he thanked his friend and set out once more on his journey. He found the walking quite easy now, and the stones did not hurt his feet. As he left the house, he remembered to look back and there, far, far away were his dear shining companions.

One day, however, the way grew much harder. They came to a swamp and the boy discovered that the way to cross it – there was no other – was to find a firm foothold on a tussock of the rough grass that grew there, and so proceed from tussock to tussock. All at once he heard a scream and saw a girl who had slipped and fallen into the mire. Leaving his tussock, he tried to pull her out and set her on her way again, and when he had shown her how to get along she glanced down at his garments: "Oh, dear," she said – they were horribly black with mud as well as being dusty from the road. Then the boy saw an old woman who could not move forward, so he helped her onto his shoulders and managed to carry her along a bit. Indeed, there were so many people to help that he forgot all about his garments and whether they were clean or dirty, until they came to the edge of the swamp and found themselves on the edge of a deep, wide river. There was no bridge and most of the people seemed afraid of trying to wade or swim over. The boy started talking to them, and said, "Why do you hesitate? You know that we all have to cross it. Come, I will go in and perhaps if you join me we shall give one another courage. I will hold your hands and go in a step ahead."

Then just before he put his feet in, he looked up and saw a hill on the further side of the river, and, as his eyes sought the top he saw, with a shock of joy, his beautiful shining companions, smiling at him and beckoning him to come to them.

He glanced down at his garments and realized how soiled they were with dust and mud.

He plunged into the river, and at first he was able to help and even support some of the people who were with him, but the river was deeper than he had thought and the current stronger and he lost his footing and found himself quite alone. It was all he could do to try to swim across the heavy current. Fainter and fainter he grew until he thought he would sink, when, at last, he felt ground under his feet and was able to climb out.

He looked up and there were his beloved companions waiting for him. He started to climb the hill and as he did so he began to feel less weary and the way seemed easier; he looked at his garments and, to his astonishment, he noticed that they were beginning to shine again. But they were not the same as they had been at the beginning of the journey for wherever they had been dusty they now began to glimmer and gleam with gold, and all along the hem and wherever they had been splashed with mud they were shining with rosy light. He wondered what his companions would have to say.

At last he stood before them and they welcomed him back to his home. The one who had sent him forth now began to speak the kindest words of welcoming to him: "When we sent you on your journey," he said, "we told you that you were to keep your garments white and shiny, but now your garments are unlike any of ours, for you have won these new colours and brought them back into our garden. We could never have done this but you have done it for us and we are grateful and welcome you back with joy into our midst."

M. Dodwell

Midsummer's Eve

Once upon a time beside a stream there stood a mill. But the rain did not fall to fill the stream, so the stream could not flow to turn the mill and the mill could not grind the corn to make bread. And the miller was sad.

Mary wanted to help the miller. On Midsummer's Eve she went out and walked beside the stream. She walked until she reached the top of the hill.

On the hilltop was a fairy ring where the fairy folk came to dance. When the sun went down the King of the Fairies led his fairy folk to dance in the ring. He saw Mary standing there. He greeted her and said: "What do you wish for, Mary?"

"I wish that the rain may fall to fill the stream, that the stream may flow to turn the mill, that the mill may grind the corn to make bread, that the miller may be happy again."

"Your wish shall be granted, Mary," said the King of the Fairies.

And the fairy folk began to dance. All night long they danced and when morning came the rain began to fall to fill the stream, and the stream began to flow to turn the mill, so the mill could grind the corn to make bread. And the miller was happy.

"Thank you, fairy folk," said Mary.

"Thank you, Mary," said the miller.

The Fairy Weaver

Once upon a time in a green valley in the hills there lived a little girl called Eileen. She lived with her father and mother on a small farm. Her father grew potatoes and kept pigs and sheep and a little grey donkey to pull the cart. Her mother spun wool from the sheep and wove it into fine cloth with patterns all along the edges in blue and green and red.

Eileen had a small room of her own underneath the roof of the cottage. When she awoke in the morning she lay in bed listening to the sparrows twittering: "Ti-wit, ti-wit, wit, wit, ti-wit," they said. Then she jumped out of bed, put on her clothes, splashed her face with cold fresh water from a wooden pail and skipped down the stairs to greet her mother with a kiss.

Under the doorstep lived a family of little mice and Eileen always put out some crumbs for them. The first thing she did in the morning was to see if they had eaten the crumbs. Sometimes they had, sometimes they hadn't and sometimes they left a small half eaten crust. Then Eileen could see the marks of their tiny teeth all around the edge.

Next she went to say good morning to the pigs, and scratched their muddy backs with a twig. The pigs loved to have their backs scratched and they grunted with pleasure when they saw Eileen coming. "Garrum, garrum, garrum," they said. Afterwards Eileen ran back into the house to have her breakfast.

After breakfast it was time for mother to begin her weaving, so Eileen helped in the house. She swept the floor, wiped the dishes, dusted and polished until everything gleamed. When she had finished she ran out to play in the meadow behind the house. There she watched the butterflies and the bees visiting the flowers and listened to the birds singing. Sometimes she followed the butterflies into the wood.

One day she wandered further into the wood than she had ever been before. She watched the work of the squirrels and the birds busy amongst the branches. Presently she came to a babbling brook and as she listened to the song of the water she heard a little voice:

"Oh dear, oh dear, what shall I do?" it said. "My shuttle has fallen into the water. What shall I do?"

Eileen looked around her and there, sitting on a fallen branch beside the brook, was the tiniest little man she had ever seen. He came no higher than her knee and he had a long grey beard which reached almost to his feet. He was looking so sadly into the water that Eileen wanted to help him.

"What is the matter?" she asked.

"My shuttle has fallen into the brook," said the little man, "I am much too small to fetch it out. I should be carried away by the water."

"I shall fetch it for you," said Eileen. There and then she took off her shoes, waded into the water and picked up the tiny shuttle from the bottom of the brook.

"Thank you, Eileen," said the little man. "If ever you are in trouble and need my help, then call on me and I shall see what I can do."

Then he sat down at his loom, which stood close by, and went on with his weaving. Eileen watched him tossing the shuttle back and forth. As she looked closely she saw that he was not weaving with wool, but with spider threads. The cloth he was weaving was finer than the finest silk and the sunbeams streaming through the branches made it shine all the colours of the rainbow. Quietly Eileen slipped away and ran all the way home.

The next day Eileen's father had to take his potatoes and some pigs to market. In the morning he harnessed the little grey donkey to the cart and loaded in the boxes of potatoes, which Eileen had helped to pick, and two small pigs. He took food and a blanket for the night. It was a long journey to the town and he would not return until the next day, bringing with him the man who would buy mother's fine cloth. So the little cart set off up the road with Eileen running alongside until she was too tired to run any more. Then she stood and waved until her father was out of sight.

When Eileen came back to the house, mother was sitting in a chair, looking tired.

"What is the matter, mother dear," asked Eileen.

"I am not well," said mother, "I think I shall go to bed."

"I shall look after you, mother," said Eileen. She took her mother a cool drink and tucked in the blankets for her. Soon she was fast asleep.

Then Eileen remembered the piece of cloth. Her mother was ill. Who could finish the weaving in time for tomorrow? She sat down and thought and thought. Then she remembered the little weaver in the woods.

Quietly she tip-toed out of the house and off she ran across the meadows. Soon she came to the brook and there sat the little man, tossing his shuttle back and forth and humming a little tune as he worked.

"Hello, Eileen," he called, "what can I do for you?"

"Mother is not well," said Eileen, "she has been weaving a piece of cloth which must be finished for tomorrow. Can you help me?"

"Do not worry," said the little man. "You go home now and you will see what you will see."

Eileen felt much happier and ran quickly home again. "Do not worry about the cloth, mother," she said. That night they both slept soundly.

In the morning Eileen didn't wait to listen to the sparrows, she ran down the stairs as fast as she could. There sat mother, quite well again, gazing at the finished piece of cloth which lay by the loom. It was the most beautifully finished piece of cloth she had ever seen. All along the edge were delicate patterns in blue and green and red.

"Who has woven the cloth so finely, Eileen?" asked mother.

"It was the little man who sits and weaves by the brook in the forest." Eileen told her mother how she had helped the little old man.

"He was one of the fairy folk," said mother. "You must not forget to thank him for his kindness to us all."

By and by father came home from market and with him came a tall man on horseback. He paid a good price for the fine piece of cloth.

Eileen told her father about the fairy weaver and then she slipped away across the meadow and into the wood. She searched high and low but nowhere could she see the little fairy man.

"Thank you, Fairy Weaver," she called. "Thank you for your help." A little breeze sprang up among the branches and the brook babbled and sang to her. Then Eileen knew that he had heard.

J. Mehta

The Green Button

Once upon a time there lived an old man. His cottage stood on the edge of the forest and he lived by himself and he kept everything tidy.

One day in the Autumn he saw that the wind had brought down the leaves. "My garden is untidy," he said. "I must gather the leaves together."

He put on his jacket and cap and boots and went outside. First he raked the lawn, then he swept the path. Suddenly he heard the clink of metal. He bent down, parted the leaves and found a small green button. He picked it up and wondered where it had come from. Then he slipped it into his pocket and said: "That will be just right for my shirt where the top button is missing,"

He put his tools into his shed and after supper he fetched the sewing basket and his shirt and sewed the button on firmly and said: "There, that will stop the wind blowing down my neck." He laid the shirt on the chair by his bed and went to sleep.

In the middle of the night he was awakened by a loud bang on the door. He got out of bed and opened the window. It was so dark that he could see nothing, but he heard a voice which shouted: "Give me back my button!" The old man quietly shut the window and went back to bed.

Two nights later he was awakened again, but this time it was by a knock, not a bang, on his door. He went downstairs and opened it. There stood a little man clad from top to toe in green and the old man noticed that the top button was missing from his coat. The little man pushed a sack towards the old man and said: "Here you are! Now give me back my button!" The old man opened the sack and saw that it was full of toadstools. Then he said gently: "These are no good to me. You keep the toadstools and I will keep the button." The old man quietly closed the door and went back to bed.

A week went by and the old man washed his clothes and the shirt with the green button too. He was hanging the washing on the line when he felt that someone stood behind him. He went on with his work and was just putting the last peg on the shirt when he heard a quiet voice say:

"Please, give me back my button." The old man turned round and said: "Now that you have asked me quietly of course I will give you back your button. Just wait while I fetch my scissors." Soon he was back with the scissors, snipped off the button and handed it to the little green man. "Thank you," he said. "You see, without it the wind blows down my neck." – "Yes, I know," said the old man, "I am sure I can find another one for my shirt."

The little green man went happily back to the forest and the old man went happily indoors.

A few days later the old man awoke one night and found his room as bright as day. He got out of bed and looked out of the window. There in the sky he saw the round full moon and when he looked down into his garden he saw a round moon on his lawn.

He quietly shut the window and went back to bed. In the morning there on the lawn was a moon of mushrooms. He went down and picked three of the largest for his breakfast. Then he stood up and called out: "Thank you, little green man! Thank you for the mushrooms." The little green man was standing behind the hedge and he smiled.

From that day on the old man found a moon of mushrooms on his lawn every year and when he had picked the first three he always stood up and said: "Thank you, little green man! Thank you for the mushrooms." And the little green man was always nearby and smiled and returned happily to the forest.

Elsie and the Seven Sheep

Once upon a time there lived a little girl named Elsie. She had neither father nor mother, nor brother nor sister, nor uncle nor aunt, nor a home to shelter her. She was pale and small with golden hair, which she kept in a plait, and this reached from her head almost to her heels. That is why she was called golden-haired Elsie.

Elsie lived on a farm with the farmer and his wife. She always made the porridge, and nobody else knew how. She always fed the chickens, and she always fetched the water from the well.

One day a queer little man came by the farm, and he brought with him some lambs for sale. "The prettiest lambs you ever saw," said the queer little man. "So they are," said the farmer. "Yes, I'll buy them. Put them in the home-field, and send golden-haired Elsie to watch them!" Then the queer little man went away.

But the queer little man had not gone an hour, before up among the hills, a horn blew clearly. The lambs stopped nibbling the grass and listened. The horn blew again once, twice, thrice - and then the lambs gave a loud "Ba - aa -," and off they went, leaping over the fence, and flying down the valley and up the hill, and were out of sight before Elsie had time to run out and scream a call for help.

Oh! Wasn't the farmer angry! Seven golden guineas had he given for those lambs, and now they were gone. And he told Elsie she was an idle, careless girl and she was never to come near him and the farm again. So Elsie went away weeping.

But presently there was trouble on the farm. The porridge was all burnt, and nobody knew why. The chickens had not been fed. Oh! Elsie always fed the chickens and everyone had forgotten them. There was no water brought from the well. Oh, no! Elsie always fetched the water.

"It seems to me," growled the farmer, "that I have sent away the only person that did any work!"

"Yes," said his wife, "that is true. And it wasn't her fault about the lambs, for I was looking out of the window, and they were all gone like a flash of lightning! You had better go and find poor Elsie, and bring her back."

But when the farmer took his wife's advice, Elsie was nowhere to be found.

Elsie had gone weeping away to look for those lambs; she could see prints of their hoofs on the soft turf, and she followed, followed, followed where the track led. Up the valley, over the hill, across the mountain brook and through the great pine wood, and when she could not see the print of their feet, lo! There were the tiny tufts of white silky wool, here and there, as if to mark the way, and at last, oh, joy! There were the seven white lambs in a tiny green field behind a quaint, brown wooden house, and when they saw her they all ran towards her. "Ba – aa, ba – aa, ba – aa," they said.

"Oh! You dear, little sheep," she cried. "Oh! Please come back with me at once," and she opened the gate and tried to drive them out of the field. But the lambs would not move.

"Hello!" cried another voice, and there was the queer little man. "What are you doing with my sheep?"

"But they are not yours," said Elsie, crossly. "You sold them to the farmer, you know you did!"

"Well, he had them," said the little man. – "But they all ran away quite directly," said Elsie.

"Ah! It is a way they have," said the little man. "But tell me what are you doing here? Has he turned you out?" – "Yes," said Elsie, wiping away a tear with her pinafore, "and if you won't let the lambs come back with me, I must find a new place."

"Ah!" said the little man, "that is lucky, for I want a new servant. Now, can you make rice puddings?"

"Oh, dear, yes!" said Elsie.

"And always sweep the stairs down on a Saturday?"

"I do that every day," remarked Elsie severely.

"And can you sew and spin, and take care of my sheep?"

"I can sew and I can spin, but 1 can't promise to take care of the sheep," cried Elsie.

"But the sheep are most particular!" said the little man, with his head on one side.

"Then I must go farther on," said Elsie, "for your sheep run too fast for me."

The little man looked at Elsie very hard. "Oh, well!" he said at last, "suppose you come and try."

So Elsie, as she had nowhere else to go, agreed she would. Now Elsie soon found that she had plenty to do in her new place. It certainly was an odd place. For, it appeared, those seven sheep quite declined to eat grass like other sheep, but required their meals regularly. First of all, Elsie had to make seven basins of bread and milk for their breakfast, and seven basins of potato soup for their dinner, and seven barley cakes for tea, and seven rice puddings for supper. As to the queer little man, he was a perfect slave to those lambs. For even if he was sitting down to a meal, and he heard the faintest "ba - aa," he was out in a moment, and he was so nervous about them at night that he never went to bed at all, but used to walk round and round the fold until he was perfectly worn out. And Elsie was so sorry for him that she got to like him very much, and, indeed, he was a kind little man, though he was so twisted and odd, and looked as if he were made of shabby leather.

"Can't you put them into the stable, and lock them up?" She asked one day.

But he shook his head sadly. "They would be out of the window in no time, if I were not there!" he answered.

But Elsie was not satisfied, and she thought and thought what she could do to keep those tiresome sheep safe, until she really could not sleep for worrying. But one night she heard someone singing, so she sat up in bed and listened, and then she could hear the words quite plainly:

> "Who in the meadow safe will keep
> The seven white sheep,
> Must go to the mere and rushes bring

> Seven time seven to plait a ring,
> And knot it fair at intervals
> With golden nodding daffodils.
> Go! Bind the garland round the fold,
> And fasten with a rope of gold.
> > That is the way those seven white sheep
> > Safe in the meadow green to keep."

Elsie was out of bed and into her clothes in a moment. Out through the still silent woods she flew, and, oh! How hard she worked, until she had plaited her garland and knotted it with flowers, and then she hurried down to the fold, where the little man was pacing round and round.

"Quick, quick," she cried, "help me to bind it round, ere the sun gets up."

But just as it was put around, she remembered she had forgotten the last thing.

"Oh!" She cried, bursting out crying, "I forgot about the rope; and it said a rope of gold. Oh! Have you any gold, master?"

"No, not a bit," said the little man.

"But perhaps something else will do. You see it goes just round, the garland does, but there is nothing left to tie. Haven't you got anything?"

"No," said the queer little man, in a squeaky voice, "there is nothing; there isn't a bit of rope or string in the place, unless, unless...."

"Unless what?" cried Elsie; but he did not answer.

"Oh! I know," cried Elsie again, for all the sheep were trying to press through the garland, and there was a grey light gleaming up the mountain. "Run quick and fetch the scissors then cut off my hair! Perhaps that will do, and it is yellow!"

"Your hair!" croaked the little man. "Oh! Not your beautiful hair!" "What does it matter?" she cried, impatiently. "Oh! Make haste, do, else the sun will be up."

"But are you quite sure you do not mind?"

"Mind! Not a bit," said Elsie, "only make haste."

Snip, snap, snip, and Elsie bound the end of her garland with her golden hair. "Good gracious!" cried Elsie.

For lo! Instead of seven white sheep, her garland held seven lovely little girls, and instead of a queer, little, wizened old man, there was a beautiful young prince, on his knees, kissing her hand, and thanking her for giving her beautiful hair, and so breaking the spell that bound him and his seven little sisters. And the brown hut was a fair palace. And the next time the farmer saw golden-haired Elsie, she and the seven little sisters came riding down the valley on white steeds, in silken robes, and paid him back the money he had given for those seven runaway lambs.

From Ireland

The Five Goats

Once there was a boy who had to look after five goats. Every morning he brought them to the meadow. There was juicy grass to eat and clear water to drink. Every evening he brought them home again and then they were milked.

One evening the goats wanted to stay in the meadow. "Hop, hop, home you go! You have to be milked," the boy called. But the goats did not go and continued eating the juicy grass.

Then his sister came and said: "Let me try. I will bring them inside." And she ran after the goats. But they did not go inside.

There came a dog walking by. "Wait, I will bring them to the stables. My voice is louder than yours: Woof! Woof! Woof" The dog ran behind the goats. But they continued eating the juicy grass and did not go inside.

There came the red fox to see why the dog was barking. "Let me try." said the fox. "The dog howls too loudly. I know something . . . . "The fox ran behind the goats and cried: "Hee-hee! Hee-hee! Inside, you goats." But the goats did not take any notice and continued eating the juicy grass.

There came the horse. "Let me fix this," said the horse. "I am bigger than the fox. I can do more than the dog and I have more legs than the boy's sister and the boy." The horse ran to the goats and called: "It is nearly dark, goats! It is time that you go to the stables." But the goats scarcely looked at the horse and continued eating juicy grass.

A bee came flying by: "What is happening here?" he asked. "Why are you still in the fields so late?" – "The goats do not want to go inside," said the boy and his sister. "Nobody can get them to the stables. The horse cannot. The fox cannot. The dog cannot. And we also cannot." – "Yes, so it is," called the horse, the fox and the dog." - "Then it is my turn," said the bee. "I will lead them inside." – "You cannot run on four legs," said the horse. "You don't know what to do," said the fox. "You cannot bark," said the dog. "You are too small," said the children. "We will see," said the bee.

He flew straight to the biggest goat and buzzed in his ear: "Bzzzzz, zoom, zoom, zoom." The goat lifted his head and saw the bee: "Oh, what is that?" cried the goat and ran away as fast as he could. "If you go inside I shall go too," said the second goat. "Then we shall all go inside," said the other goats. And so the bee led the five goats into the stables.

From Holland

A Bubble Story

> Waterfall Lady falling down
> With thousand bubbles in your crown.
> Laugh your bubbles round and cool
> Big and small into the pool.
> Bubbles, bubbles, floating down the stream . . .
> Bubbles, bubbles, tell your rainbow dream.

This is a story about a bubble, a little bubble. In fact it was the littlest bubble ever seen.

"I am so small," the littlest bubble whispered as he left his bubbly waterfall mother and floated down the stream with all the other bubbles. "Look at my bubble brothers and bubble sisters, they have big rainbow dreams. My rainbow dream can hardly be seen."

The bubbles floated down the country stream, past green willows and grass rushes, past large brown cows, past platypus burrows and rabbit furrows, around hills and through valleys. On and on until they came to the edge of a green field. They heard the voices of children who were picnicking in the shade of a tree.

"Look," a boy called out, "bubbles! Let's catch them."

"Bubbles!" called out the other children, and they jumped up and ran to the edge of the stream:

> "Bubbles, bubbles, the biggest bubbles ever seen,
> Bubbles, bubbles, and here we catch a rainbow dream."

Soon all the big bubbles were gone. They were no more than a wish in the children's hand, no more than a rainbow for the children to take to dreamland.

And what about the littlest bubble? The children had not seen him, the children had not caught his rainbow dream. So there he was, all alone, floating down the stream.

"Why," he thought, "I am so little and so I did not get caught."

On and on he floated, until the stream reached the sea. And there the waves took him out into the blue, far out where the sea-fairies danced and played.

One sea-fairy was busy stirring a pot of pearl when the littlest bubble floated by, and his littlest rainbow dream caught the sea-fairy's eye. "Just what I need to colour my pot of pearl," the sea-fairy said. And she picked him up and popped him in. And with a this-way whirl and a that-way swirl the littlest bubble helped to make a pot of rainbow pearl.

S. Perrow

St. John's Gift

In a far off country lay three cornfields next to each other. In all three fields grew corn, yet each looked different. In the first field the weeds grew freely and suffocated the corn. In the second field there was not a single weed or flower to be seen amongst the corn. In the third field there were some red poppies and some blue corn-flowers which looked beautiful together with the yellow corn.

In this country, harvest was before St. John's Day and so the farmers came out to cut their corn. The first farmer was a real careless Jack; whistling, he cut his corn and did not notice that he was cutting more flowers and weeds than corn, nor that he had forgotten some sheaves on the field, and neither did he notice that some sheaves fell off the cart because he had loaded it badly. At home he threshed the corn that was left over and put it into his damp and dirty barn. He was glad that the corn was out of his sight.

The farmer of the second field, which did not have a single weed, was a greedy man. He mowed his field as carefully as possible and he did not leave a single stalk standing. Then, as if by mistake, he mowed a small strip of corn from the third field and another small strip of corn and yet another one, and put the corn with his own. On the way home he ran along the wagon and made sure that not a single grain was lost. At home he counted the sheaves and, when he had threshed the corn, he swept each single grain up and locked and bolted the barn himself.

Then came the third farmer. He was sorry that some of his corn had already been mown but he did not make a fuss. Happily he mowed his corn and his children made beautiful posies of the poppies and corn-flowers. Singing, they went home and the mother came to help with the threshing and the whole family put the corn into the barn.

Now, in this country, every year on St. John's Day, a big fire was lit outside the village, and all the farmers came and scattered a handful of the new corn into the fire as a gift to St. John and only after they had done this, would they bake and cook and eat the new corn.

It happened that a few days before St. John's Day a beggar boy walked through the village. He looked hungry and tired as if he had come from afar.

He went from house to house and asked for a piece of bread. Then he came to careless Jack. Careless Jack was not even thinking of St. John's Day and the fire, and as he did not have any old corn and old flour he went into the barn to get some new corn to bake bread for the beggar boy. But alas, in the damp and dirty barn the new corn had already begun to rot and could not be used. Sadly the beggar boy walked on and knocked on the door of the greedy farmer.

The greedy farmer shouted at the beggar boy angrily: "Don't you know that we have not had the St. John's fire yet and given our gift of a handful of new corn to the fire? How dare you ask for bread!" He did not say that his wife was just baking a cake out of the new corn. Sadly, the beggar boy walked on and knocked on the door of the third farmer.

The third farmer, too, was thinking of the St. John's fire and of the St. John's gift. But when he saw the tired and hungry child he welcomed him in and said to his wife: "Although we have not yet given our handful of grain to the fire for St. John we cannot let anybody suffer hunger." So he took some new corn, ground it, and his wife baked a good cake. Then the farmer and his wife and children sat down with the beggar boy together, and in order that he should not eat by himself they each had a small piece of cake too. When the boy had had enough they wrapped the cake up and put it into his sack, for his journey.

St. John's Day came. The three farmers walked together to the place where the St. John's fire was to be lit. Each carried in his hand a small sack of new corn. It was evening and the evening mist settled over the valley. The mist and clouds grew thicker and thicker so that the three farmers could no longer see their hands in front of their faces. And then . . . . .how strange . . . . . the path began to get steeper and steeper – had they lost their way? Higher and higher the path took them and at last they came out above the mist and clouds. The evening sun was bright again and shone onto the white clouds below them. When they looked up they saw that they stood in front of three great doors of heaven: one very great one in the middle and a smaller one on either side. In front of the great middle gate, stood a man with fair hair who looked like the sun himself.

Kindly he said: "My friends, what do you wish to bring me?" The greedy farmer wanted to keep the corn for himself and shouted: "Nothing for you, we are bringing our gift for St. John!" "Then you may give it to me for I am St. John," said the fair figure. Frightened, the greedy man tightened his lips.

Careless Jack ran and pressed forward to the fair figure and gave him his sack. St. John opened it and shook his head sadly: "This corn is half rotten and not good enough for him who lives behind the great gate and who is to receive it." Thereupon the small gate on the left side opened and careless Jack saw a hissing snake. He had to feed his rotten corn to the snake and the gate closed behind him.

Then it was the greedy farmer's turn to hand his new corn to St. John. When the fair figure opened the sack and saw black grains, he shook his head sadly: "Stolen goods don't grow." Thereupon the small gate on the right side opened and the greedy farmer saw a yellow-green dragon. He had to feed his black grains to the dragon and the gate closed behind him. And now it was the third farmer's turn. He hardly dared to offer his new corn to St. John. When the fair figure opened the sack a bright radiance shone forth: the grains had become gold!

St. John asked: "With whom have you shared your bread?"

"With wife and children," said the farmer, "and a poor beggar boy who came to our house."

The face of St. John lit up with joy, and he said: "You have given the true gift." Then the great gate in the middle opened and a light as bright as the morning sun shone forth.

There stood Mother Mary and the Christ Child. Said the Christ Child in his bright voice to the farmer: "I thank you for taking me into your house when I came as a beggar boy and for sharing your bread with me. Give me your corn now that it may be blessed." Then the Christ Child shared the corn which had been blessed with the farmer and said: "Take this half with you, it is yours." When the farmer came home he ground the handful of grain the Christ Child had given him, and his wife baked a loaf of bread. They ate it with their children and gave to all hungry people too. And as long as they lived this bread lasted and never grew less.

U. de Haes

The Golden Bucks

Once upon a time there lived a king who went out hunting. The whole day long he rode over the wild heath, but did not see any game. Then towards evening he tethered his horse to a tree and sat down on a hillock, tired and discouraged. Suddenly he perceived a golden buck up in the crags and clefts of the mountains. The animal looked proud and majestic, he had golden horns and a golden coat and it seemed as if glittering pearls hung from each hair. In the glow of the evening sun the king's eyes hurt with beholding such beauty.

"If only this buck were mine, then I would be happy," the king said, and gazed and gazed until he could gaze no more. He returned home late that evening and still the golden buck stood before his eyes and he could not get any peace.

Then the king had it proclaimed in all the churches of his kingdom that he who could catch the golden buck would receive his daughter and half his kingdom, "but he who cannot must either spend a night in the ghost house or be tied to a post and have strips cut from his back," said the king.

Understandably, many wanted to win the king's daughter. Knights, young lords and princes pronounced themselves ready - all those people who thought they were better than others, but how ill they all fared! They saw neither hide nor hair of this golden buck and returned from the king's castle with sore backs, or half mad after a night with ghosts.

Now there was a man who had two sons, the eldest of whom wanted to set out. "Dear child, of what use is that?" said the father, "either you will return as a madman or with a skinned back." But whatever the father said it was of no avail, the son was determined to go. He received a knapsack with some bread and went forth.

He came to a hut where an old man was sitting outside, mending his clothes. The boy sat down by him and took off his knapsack and began to eat.

"Have you perchance a bit for me too?" enquired the old man, "I am so hungry."

No, he did not have anything for the old man, the boy said. "I am seeking the golden buck for the king and that could take a longtime, I need the bread for myself."

"Well, you will surely find the golden buck! You will surely be king!" mocked the old man laughing. The boy wandered on and arrived at the king's castle and offered to find the golden buck.

"Very well," said the king. He would have to gather all his wits together and the conditions – well he surely knew them. The boy went forth.

When he had climbed the mountain where the king had seen the buck he suddenly perceived the shadow of a giant with a horn in his hand. And while the boy stood and gaped the giant began to blow the horn and the sound resounded through the nooks and crannies and three golden bucks sprang out and surrounded the giant. The boy was so happy as he climbed from rock to rock, believing he had fulfilled his task. But when he had climbed higher, there before him was an iron fence barring his way, and inside the railings lay a monstrous dragon, ready to devour anybody who approached. The boy was frightened and took to his heels. But the dragon had already seen him and spat venom and poison after him, hurting the boy's back and blistering his skin.

"Well, how did you fare?" asked the king on his return to the castle yard.

"Oh, God have mercy!" said the boy, "no human being can reach the summit! No less than three bucks are there but around the mountain where they graze is a high iron fence with a lock and inside lies a dragon with jaws so large that he can devour four men all at once. He saw me and I fled while he spat venom and poison after me that will leave scars for the rest of my life," he said.

"Which punishment will you choose?" asked the king.

"Have I not been punished enough?" said the boy and showed his back.

"Strips from your back or into the ghost house with you," said the king.

In the morning the boy staggered home, very disturbed. On the way, later in the day, he came to the hut of the old man. "And the golden buck?" asked the old man. But the boy would give no answer. "Oh dear, and how I rejoiced, hoping to see you as the chosen and crowned one," he mocked, "but now you come back as though you had been boiled." Still the boy would give no answer but staggered on.

His father was filled with sorrow when he saw him again, so tattered and badly treated, but nothing could be done about it now. "It would have been better if I had gone," said the little brother.

"Small boys like you who sit in cosy corners can never get there," said the other, making fun of him.

"Tomorrow I shall go," said the little brother.

"Oh no, you will not," said the father. But to talk to him was of no use, so he took a knapsack with some bread and wine and off he went. "When you come home I will have to deal with two madmen," said his father.

Later in the day the boy reached the hut where the old man lived. He went in, greeted him and asked if he might sit down at the table to eat. The old man said nothing. "Do you feel like something to eat? If so, come and join me," said the boy.

"Many thanks," said the old man, "very seldom do I get offered food."

The boy took his bottle and gave the man a drink. "Now, it is exactly one and a half hundred years ago since I last tasted wine," said he smacking his lips and enjoying the meal. "Such a kind boy has never been here before, and because of that I will help you."

When they had eaten, they went outside. The man took down a long black pipe which hung on the wall and he blew on it. The sound was louder than any the boy had ever heard. Then the old man gazed in front of him for a long time and cleared his throat, "hum, hum." Then he blew again. "What can the matter be? Why does she not come?" he said. And then he blew for the third time, so hard that nobody had ever heard the like of it — even the mountains and hillocks seemed to shake. At last a goose came flying towards them. "Where have you been?" asked the man.

"I was so faraway that I did not hear you," answered the goose, "but what do you want of me?"

"You will accompany this boy to the giantess of Niponut, you know the way well," he said. Then the man fetched an old trough, "Sit in it!" he said to the boy.

"But is it not too small?" asked the boy.

"Sit down. Leave the rest to me." The boy sat down in the trough and suddenly it became a big boat, that could easily have carried a score of men. Then the man told him what he had to do once he reached the giantess. And so they set out, the goose in front. Sometimes she swam, sometimes she flew and the boy in his boat always followed behind. After a while they reached a huge mountain. This was the home of the giantess.

"Now you go in while I stay outside," said the goose and gave him the key to the room. The boy took the large key – how heavy it was! He unlocked the door and went inside.

"Good day," said the giantess. "What do you want here?" she said.

"I only wanted to enquire if you need a shepherd," said the boy.

"Can you guard sheep?" asked the woman.

"Yes, that is a trade I learned well," answered the boy. The giantess liked the boy. She came nearer and nearer to him and started chatting to him.

"We have three golden bucks," she said, "my husband is guarding them high upon the summit. If you can manage that you can stay." That did not seem too difficult a job, thought the boy. "We could become good friends," said the horrible, ugly giantess. "My husband, you know, has been drinking too much lately and then he is wild with me," she said.

"Yes, I would like to," said the boy, although he was frightened. 'No better way to find out everything I need to know,' he thought, and so they became good friends.

She told him about shepherding, about the meadow and the giant, the dragon and the poison-sack, and more. "But how is it possible to get the poison-sack, which he has under his tongue?" asked the boy.

"When the dragon is asleep, you can take it," she said.

"Well, when does he sleep?" asked the boy.

"Exactly at the sound of the bell; I can't be quite sure, but when the sun stands highest in the sky, that is when he sleeps."

"Well, now I'm really frightened of the beast," said the boy.

"Do as I told you, then you need not worry," said she, and thereupon she fetched a jug of ale. "You must be thirsty," she said, and begged him to drink. The boy dared not refuse and so he pretended to drink, but really he let everything run into his clothes.

"So, now I'm ready," said the boy, thanked her for the food and drink, put the knapsack on his back and went out.

"May all go well with you," she called. Outside stood the goose, and when the boy came out she asked:

"Have you managed your task?"

"Yes, I have managed," he said and climbed into the boat and away they went. In no time at all they were back with the old man in his hut. And he was curious and wanted to know how the boy and the goose had fared with the giantess of Niponut. And the boy told him all.

"So, now go to the castle of the king and say why you have come. Then ask the king for bread and a jug of good wine, but the jug must not be too small, do you understand?"

When the boy reached the castle, the king was just walking across the courtyard, throwing his hands up and conducting himself in his usual manner. The boy told him what he wanted to do, but although this made him happy he thought the boy too small and young to fulfill such a great task. Meanwhile, the king's daughter came walking by; she saw the boy and liked him, and wished that good fortune might accompany him.

The boy received the food and drink for which he had asked and went forth. When he came to the hut, he went in and refreshed the old man with food and drink. "Soon the sun will be high in the sky," said the old man, "it would be best if you went on your way now." Then the old man put something in the boy's hand. It looked like salt. "This you must give to the bucks," said he, "then they will become so tame that they will run after you like lambs." He blew once more on his flute and the goose appeared. "When you get to the iron fence and have unlocked it, it will be best if the goose takes the poison-sack as she is very nimble. And after that you know what to do," said the old man.

Then they went on their way like lightning, the goose ahead and the boy behind, until they came to the iron fence. The boy turned the key in the lock and there lay the dragon, snoring. He slept with his mouth wide open; it was a terrible sight. The goose quickly took the poison-sack from the dragon's mouth and passed it to the boy. The dragon awoke, rolled and wriggled and flung his tail about until it seemed that the earth would open. There he lay, struggling and puffing until he bled to death. "Now I no longer need to stay," said the goose. "I will leave you the boat, it knows the way by itself." Then they parted, the goose went on her way and the boy climbed up the wooden ladder, in one hand the poison-sack and in the other the jug.

High upon the mountain sat the giant blowing his horn. "Good day," said the boy greeting him respectfully.

"God bless you," said the giant with a rough voice. "What do you want here?"

"I want to help you tend your flock," said the boy.

"How on earth did you get past the dragon?" asked the giant.

"Well, he knew that I wanted to help you tend your flock," answered the boy.

That impressed the giant and he started talking to the boy in a friendly way. "What's your name, you little chap?" he asked him.

"Love," answered the boy, "and yours?"

"Mine? I have the same name as my grandfather," said the giant.

"1 have a good drink with me," said the boy, "do you want to try it?" And he passed him the jug and the giant drank.

After a while they set out and climbed higher up the mountains. Then the giant took his horn and blew on it and at the same time the golden bucks came running. "What am I doing! Now I have blown the wrong tune," he said. He had three tunes, he told the boy; one for the bucks to run in the morning into the wood; one for them to go and eat, and one for coming home at night. But now it was not yet time for the bucks to be looked after and so he warbled them away again.

"You do have magnificent bucks," said the boy.

"Yes, 1 think so, too," said the giant, "there are none like them in this country, not in eighteen kingdoms, and I won't give any away."

"No, no, that cannot be expected of you," said the boy. "Please be so good as to teach me your tunes, without them I cannot look after your three bucks."

"Yes, true enough, I will do that," said the giant, and began with the morning tune. When he blew the third tune, the bucks came straight away.

"Please let me try your pipe," said the boy, and then he piped and warbled the bucks to him and away from him, just as the master had done. Then he gave the bucks some of his salt and they became so tame and trusting that they followed him wherever he went.

"Have you still something left in your jug, Love?" asked the giant. The boy gave him the jug and the giant drank the rest of the wine. Then he wanted to show off, and he grasped a huge pine tree and bent it right down to its roots as though it were a twig. "Yes, yes, we chaps in Niponut, we can use our fists, don't you think?" he said. Then he stamped about and uprooted trees. But soon his head became heavy and then heavier. He sat down and mumbled and grumbled and gurgled and fell asleep. Then smoke and steam rose from his mouth and a blue flame appeared. And the smoke and flame grew so strong that embers, ash and smoke gushed out. The boy took the poison-sack and thrust it into the giant's mouth and the giant was scattered into a hundred pieces, so that nothing remained that might have resembled him.

Then the boy called the bucks and they followed him as they had once done the giant. They got down to the boat and sailed homeward, and it was not long before they found themselves with the old man in the hut. "Now all is well and right," said the man. "You will travel to the king's castle with the bucks and then you will receive the king's daughter."

When the boy arrived at the castle, the king was greatly surprised at seeing the three golden bucks and he welcomed the boy with great honour.

The wedding feast was prepared and there was so much to eat and drink that all who were present said that they had never been to such a splendid feast before.

And when the king died the prince and princess received the whole kingdom, and lived for many happy years.

From Norway

The Sun Castle

In the middle of a huge forest there once lived a farmer. In front of his house stretched a meadow with many flowers, and the most beautiful grass that could be found far and wide grew there.

This meadow seemed to him the most precious possession he had. How great, therefore, was his astonishment when on a clear Summer's morning he observed that the grass had been trampled down. "Who could that have been?" said the farmer to himself. On the following morning he stood again very early in front of his house and again the grass lay broken and trampled down on the ground. This could only have happened during the night. Filled with anger and grief he made up his mind to find out who could have caused him such harm. He ordered his eldest son to keep watch during the night and to observe who walked through the grass.

The son sat down behind a bush on the edge of the wood, but at about midnight he felt so tired that he sank into a deep sleep. He slept like a dormouse and only awoke as the sun was shining onto the mountains of Tessin, bathing them in pure gold. He rubbed his eyes and saw that the meadow had been trampled down, just as before. Ashamed and angry, he returned to the house, unable to give his father an explanation.

The following night the farmer gave the task of watching the meadow to his second son. He promised to find out, without fail, who the wrongdoer might be. He said goodnight to his parents and hid in the bushes. But he, too, sank into a deep sleep and slumbered like a lazy-bones, so that in the morning he had to go home without success.

When the third son heard this he offered to watch for the third night. "That is love's labour lost," replied his father, "you are still to young to keep watch outside for a whole night! And in any case you won't be any more successful than your brothers." But the youngest son begged and pleaded until his father consented. When it became dark, he slipped into the forest meadow. There he watched the whole night but nothing happened. He began to get impatient, but stayed at his post. At last, the sun rose over the mountains and there he saw, in the dim twilight, three snow white doves descend. After a short rest, they laid their feathered dresses on the grass and changed into three maidens. They then performed on the meadow the most enchanting dance, so light and gentle, like fairies, with feet hardly touching the flowered carpet.

One of the three maidens was so beautiful that the youngest son, Vittorino, could not resist her loveliness and a great love for her grew in his heart. He crept out and secretly took their fine feathered clothes and hid behind a hedge of wild roses. In the meantime the sun had risen higher and gilded the tree-tops of the forest. Now the maidens realised that the time had come to stop dancing. They ran to pick up their coats, but could not find them. They searched here and there, and at last discovered the youth under the rose bush. Immediately they suspected, and rightly so, that he had taken their clothes. They approached him in the most courteous manner and begged him kindly to give back their feather clothes. "I will bring them to you," replied the youth, "but on two conditions. First of all you must tell me who you are and where you come from."

"Very well, listen then," the most beautiful of them replied. "I am the only daughter of a mighty king and these are my playmates and maids of honour. We come from the Sun Castle where no human has ever set foot, and nobody can get there."

"My second condition," the youth continued, "is that the princess will give me her love and be true forever. She herself shall name the day of our wedding." When the three maidens realized how high the sun had risen and how the day was becoming bright, they had no choice but to agree also to the second condition. Thereupon the two lovers pledged to be true for ever more, named the day of their wedding and promised never to leave one another. Now Vittorino gave them back their feather dresses, the maidens changed back into doves and flew away over the forest meadow. Hardly had Vittorino entered the house, when his father and brothers showered him with questions. But he spoke little and pretended that he had sunk into a deep sleep and had noticed nothing. The brothers laughed at him for having tried to outdo them.

At last came the longed-for day on which the wedding would be celebrated. Vittorino went to his father and requested from him a promise to arrange a big feast and to invite all their friends and relations.

And so it happened.

The finest food and best wines were delivered. Through the happy noise of clinking glasses, the sound of a coach was suddenly heard. It drove into the courtyard, pulled by four stately horses. From it stepped the beautiful princess dressed in a wonderful wedding gown and accompanied by her two ladies-in-waiting.

When the guests were told the truth about that magical night, they congratulated the youth and could not take their eyes away from the beautiful bride. And so the wedding was celebrated with much joy.

But before the dawn rose over the forest meadow, the bride said: "Now I must hasten away and return to my castle, because 1 am being watched by Orco, an evil magician. He must not find out about my secret wedding or he would strangle me, wheresoever I might be." The young bridegroom dared not prevent her journey, although his heart was breaking. Instead he urged her to hurry, so that no harm might befall her. With tears in their eyes they said farewell, and when they embraced for the last time, the bride gave him a precious ring for a keepsake. Then she climbed with her ladies-in-waiting into the golden coach, and away rolled the carriage as fast as the wind.

From that day Vittorino could find no rest. He wished for nothing else, but to get to the Sun Castle. So one day he went to his father with the request to leave. His father did not want to stand in his son's way and gave his blessing. So the youth went forth and asked everywhere he went where the Sun Castle could be, but nobody could tell him the right way. He reached a forest and there heard two mighty voices, whose echoes resounded from the mountains and the gullies of the wild rivers. Carefully he went on and caught sight of two giants who were quarrelling with one another. He took courage, stepped forward, and asked them: "Why are you fighting with each other?" Then one of them answered:

"Our father died not so long ago, and so my brother and I shared his belongings. Now we are only left with a pair of shoes, a cloak and a sword to be shared. And each of us wants these things for himself."

"Well then," replied Vittorino, "if you can't agree, I will make a suggestion. And if you follow my advice, I assure you that afterwards you will have back your peace and will love each other like good brothers." When the two giants heard the suggestion, they begged him to explain himself in more detail. "Well, my friends, I am a poor wanderer and must travel far, through kingdoms, across high mountains and must overcome many dangers. If you give me your cloak, your shoes and your sword, they will be of great service to me, and you need not quarrel over them any more."

The two giants liked the idea, and they gave him the three items as a present. "But now, young man, before you go on your way, you must learn what properties the presents possess. When you put on these shoes with each step you will walk a hundred miles. The cloak will make you invisible to your enemies. And, if you touch somebody with the point of this sword, he will drop down dead, yet if you touch the forehead of a dead person with the hilt of the sword, he will come to life again."

Vittorino put on the seven-league boots forthwith, wrapped the cloak around him, girded on his sword, thanked the giants and took his leave.

He was full of joy and wandered through unknown lands and towns, over plains, rivers and mountains.

One night he came to a thick forest. Tired by the journey he wanted to lie down, but just then he saw a light between the trees in the distance. He gathered all his strength, walked towards the light and reached a poor hut. An old woman sat in front of the door. Vittorino took off his hat, greeted the woman with kind words and begged her to put him up for the night because he could not go any further. She asked him to come in, and before he went to sleep he asked her if she knew where the Sun Castle was to be found. "Tomorrow morning," answered the old woman, "I will summon my subjects and ask them where this castle may be. Now good night, handsome youth."

As soon as the sun rose over the mountains, the old woman called all the animals of the wood to her, because they were her subjects. Soon there gathered in front of her cottage, bears, wolves, tigers, lions, panthers and all kinds of animals, lying peacefully at the feet of their mistress. The old woman asked them where the Sun Castle might be found. The animals took counsel, but none could give any information. "As you can see," said the old woman, "it is impossible for me to show you the way. But I have a sister who lives a hundred-thousand miles from here. She rules over the fish, and is the queen of the inhabitants of the rivers, lakes and oceans. It is possible that she may know something." Vittorino was not discouraged, and he thanked her and wandered on. In the evening he reached the shore of the ocean. There, he saw on the beach a broken-down hut, and on the doorstep he found a woman who was of great age and more bent than the first one. He greeted her respectfully, told her the reason for his journey and begged her to let him stay the night, which she allowed him to do.

At the break of dawn, she sat down by the waves of the sea and called her many thousands of subjects to her and asked them where the Sun Castle might be found. All the inhabitants came swimming along, the whales, the dolphins, the salmon, the pike and many others and took counsel.

After a lengthy discussion they agreed that nobody had yet heard of a castle of that name. The old woman was sorry because she could not help the young man but, she added: "Many miles from here there lives my eldest sister. She is the queen of all the birds and perhaps she can give you more information. And if she too does not know anything, further questioning will be in vain. Farewell." Vittorino thanked her and wandered many more miles. Then he spent the night in a dark grotto of the mountains. The next morning he saw on the summit of the mountain ridge a fallen-down hut. Next to it stood an old woman who was warming herself in the sun. He climbed up to her, greeted her and kissed her wrinkled hand. Who could know how many years she had spent in this mountain solitude?

"Who are you?" the woman, who was over a hundred years old, asked in a solemn voice. "You must know that I have never seen a human face on these mountains. You are the first, so please be welcome and tell me what brings you here."

"For a long time now I have been wandering through countries and towns, searching for the beautiful Sun Castle, to which nobody has yet been able to go," answered Vittorino.

"Be comforted, my dear. I do not know which path leads to it but the birds over which I rule may be able to show you the way." And with that she called all the birds together with a shepherd's pipe. There came eagles, vultures, falcons, storks, doves and blue-green parrots, all of which settled at the feet of their mistress. "I have called you to me," she said, "to find out if one of you knows the way to the Sun Castle." The birds held counsel but declared, after much chirping, that such a castle was unknown to them. "But are you all here?" she asked impatiently. "Where is the phoenix?"

After a long wait there came yet another bird which, exhausted as he was, sank to the ground. It was the phoenix. The old woman asked him sternly why he had made them wait so long. "Don't be angry, dear mistress," answered the bird, "and please excuse me, I could not be here any sooner because, can you imagine it, I have this moment come from the Sun Castle."

"Well, now," replied the queen, "you will have to fly back and be a guide for this youth."

Vittorino took his leave with many thanks to the old woman, settling himself on the back of the big bird. They flew upwards through the clouds and soon saw the mountains, valleys and oceans disappear below them.

At last they reached the Sun Castle where the bird set the rider gently down on the steps of the golden palace and Vittorino thanked him a thousand times.

Night had already fallen when he knocked on the door.

One of the ladies-in-waiting who had danced in the forest meadow appeared and, frightened by the sight of the youth, she ran back into the house. Thereupon he knocked again and this time the other opened the door.

Surprised by the sight of the youth, she, too, hurried back to her mistress, to tell her the news. It wasn't long before his lovely bride appeared, accompanied by her two ladies-in-waiting.

Vittorino handed his loved one the ring as a sign of recognition, upon which she straight away let the portal of the castle be opened. She rushed towards her bridegroom, embraced and kissed him, and begged him to come in. Vittorino told her about all his adventures in his search for the Sun Castle.

His beautiful bride was in great fear of the magician Orco, who had killed her father and brothers, so as to win the princess as his wife, and Orco watched her day and night.

Next morning when Orco came to the castle, he immediately noticed that all was not well and spoke:

> "Softly will I creep along
> Thus to catch him with my prong."

Vittorino, though, had seen him and quickly wrapping himself in the invisible cloak, stood by the hall door. At the very moment that Orco stepped over the threshold, the youth struck him with the magic sword such a blow that the monster fell dead to the ground. Now that the bride and bridegroom were free of their worst enemy, the two embraced. The youth received all the honours of a knight, as such a brave and noble hero deserved.

Yet one last thing was missing to complete the princess' happiness. She thought of her dear father and brothers who would have liked to rejoice with her but had become the victims of the dreadful Orco. Then the bridegroom was led to the tomb in which the dead had only recently been laid to rest and Vittorino lifted the lid of the coffins to touch the dead with the hilt of his sword. Lo and behold, they awoke to new life!

Thereupon the brave knight was crowned king and the wedding feast celebrated once more. Vittorino loved his beautiful bride above all measure. He ruled with wisdom and kindness and he did not forget his parents and brothers, but let them share his wealth.

And so he and his lovely wife lived a long and happy life in the Sun Castle.

From Switzerland

Recommended Reading

A is for Ox, B. Sanders ISBN 9780679417118 Pantheon Books
Failure to Connect, J. Healy, Simon & Schuster
Set Free Childhood, M. Large ISBN 9781903458433 Hawthorn Press
Rudolf Steiner, R. Lissau ISBN 9781903458563 Hawthorn Press
Lifeways, G. Davy & B. Voors ISBN 9780950706245 Hawthorn Press
The Spiritual Tasks of the Homemaker, M. Schmidt-Brabant
    ISBN 9780904693843 Temple Lodge Publishing, England
Education Towards Freedom ISBN 9780863156519
    Floris Press, Edinburgh, Scotland
Work and Play in Early Childhood, F. Jaffke
    ISBN 9780863152276 Floris Books
Festivals, Family and Food, D. Carey & J. Large
    ISBN 9780950706238 Hawthron Press
Festivals Together, S. Fitzjohn, M. Weston & J. Large
    ISBN 9781869890469 Hawthorn Press
Understanding Children's Drawings, M. Strauss ISBN 9781855841994
    Rudolf Steiner Press, England
The Wisdom of Fairytales, R. Meyer ISBN 9780863152085 Floris Books
A Guide to Child Health, M. Glöckler & W. Goebel
    ISBN 9780863159671 Floris Books
Education as Preventive Medicine – A Salutogenic Approach,
    M Glöckler, Rudolf Steiner College Press, California, USA.
Between Form and Freedom, B Staley ISBN 9781903458891 Hawthorn Press
Brothers and Sisters, K. König, Floris Books
The Challenge of the Will, Margret Meyerkort & Rudi Lissau,
    Rudolf Steiner College Press
The Oxford Nursery Songbook,
    ISBN 9780193301931 Oxford University Press
The Oxford Dictionary of Nursery Rhymes
    ISBN 9780198600886 Oxford University Press

Let us Form a Ring,
    WECAN Waldorf Early Childhood Association of North America
The Book of 1000 Poems ISBN 9780001855083
    HarperCollins Children's Books
English Fairy Tales, J. Jacobs
The Complete Grimm's Fairy Tales ISBN 9780394709307 Random House
Milly Molly Mandy Books, J. Lankester Brisley, Puffin Books
Seven-Year-Old Wonder Book, I. Wyatt ISBN 9780863159435 Floris Books

Acknowledgements

Further to the acknowledgement on page 3 of this book, the following is a list of permissions granted to reproduce previously published copyright material. Where it has not been possible to locate the original copyright holder, we tender our apologies to any owner whose rights may have been unwittingly infringed.

Ay-a little bird, by Alois Künstler is reproduced from Das Brünnlein singt und saget by kind permission of Verlag Freies Geistesleben, Stuttgart, Germany. From HarperCollins Publishers Ltd, we are grateful to reproduce the following items from The Book of 1000 Poems: The farmer is busy – titled Haymaking – by E M Adams, and Here we come A-Haying by Eunice Close. The little green frog – titled The Frog – by Rose Fyleman is reproduced by permission of The Society of Authors as the literary representative of the Estate of Rose Fyleman.

Wynstones Press

Wynstones Press publishes and distributes a range of books, including many titles for children, parents and teachers.

Also available is a wide selection of postcards, folded cards and prints reproduced from original work by a variety of artists. Included amongst these are many works by David Newbatt, who illustrated the covers for this book.

Wynstones Press also distributes a selection of beautifully illustrated Advent Calendars, from publishers in Europe.

For further information please contact:

Wynstones Press
Ruskin Glass Centre
Wollaston Road
Stourbridge
West Midlands DY8 4HE.
England.

Email: info@wynstonespress.com
Website: wynstonespress.com